Chill Out Fido!

How to Calm Your Dog

Nan Kené Arthur, CDBC, CPDT, KPACTP

Dogwise™ Publishing

Wenatchee, Washington U.S.A.

Chill Out Fido!
How to Calm Your Dog
Nan Arthur

Dogwise Publishing
A Division of Direct Book Service, Inc.
403 South Mission Street, Wenatchee, Washington 98801
509-663-9115, 1-800-776-2665
www.dogwisepublishing.com / info@dogwisepublishing.com
© 2009 Nan Arthur

Photos: Mike Arthur, Nan Arthur, Madeline Gabriel
Graphic Design: Lindsay Peternell

Portions of the exercise "The Doorbell Rings—Just a Minute" first appeared on www.clickertraining.com. Used with permission.

Library of Congress Cataloging-in-Publication Data
   Arthur, Nan Kene, 1954-
   Chill out fido! : how to calm your dog / by Nan Kene Arthur.
   p. cm.
   Includes bibliographical references and index.
   ISBN 978-1-929242-63-4
   1. Dogs--Training. I. Title.
   SF431.A78 2009
   636.7--dc22
   2009004154

ISBN13: 978-1-929242-63-4

Printed in the U.S.A. on recycled paper.

DEDICATION

To Mike—my amazing husband whose
support has been a rock.

To Madeline Gabriel, CPDT—one of the finest,
most patient teachers I've ever known.

Lest I forget the dog that brought me to life as I know it,
Codi Blu (RIP), who taught me patience.

TABLE OF CONTENTS

ACKNOWLEDGMENTS

I'm forever grateful for the fortitude and faith that the good people at Dogwise Publishing provided in helping to mold and shape the outcome of this book. Their gentle pushes and suggestions made this all come together.

Without the insight and help of many teachers along the way, this book would have only been a dream. The dogs, of course, have been the greatest teachers of all—each one an education, but it was my Australian Shepherd Codi Blu (my first dog as an adult), who started me on the path to becoming a positive reinforcement trainer. It didn't begin that way with Codi, but her sensitive nature and wicked-smart intelligence showed me there was a far better way than punishment and corrections. Rest in peace, Codi.

From the human sector, Bernice Friedman and her husband Norman moved me further into my trade by convincing me to volunteer with the rescue group they supported at the time. To say I was "roped" in would be an understatement, but the knots of that rope were always loose and these two wonderful people (along with the help of many other volunteers) gently guided me toward my career as a professional dog trainer and behavior consultant.

As the Manager of the San Diego Humane Society at the time, Madeline Gabriel, CPDT took me under her knowledgeable and sturdy wing and hired me as her Senior Behavior Trainer. It was under her supervision and tutelage that my skills as an instructor flourished. She is one of the gentlest and most effective trainers I have ever met. She has a talent for thinking in parallel with dogs (and other animals). I learned that there was never a need for anything other than positive methods of training and behavior modification. Madeline's current specialty, Dogs and Babies, has expanded my horizons even further with the identification of the similarities between raising peaceable dogs and children.

Other people who helped me broaden my dog skills include Sara Mullen; Kyle Rayon, CPDT; and Margaret Lenoir, CPDT. These remarkable women bestowed their insight of dog behavior upon me and taught me much over the years. Without each of them sharing their training talents and ideas, I doubt I would have learned the intrinsic subtleties needed to write this book.

The next generation of dog trainers will include young people like my associate Jessica Wheatcraft, CDT. Trainers like Jessica will move positive reinforcement to a completely new level for dogs and humans as they coexist. I'm blessed to have such wonderful support from Jessica.

I would also like to say thank you to my friends and clients for volunteering themselves and their dogs for photos.

Finally, to Karen Pryor whose book, *Don't Shoot the Dog!*, was one of the early books I found when trying to solve my dog Codi's behavior problems. Reading it prevented me from "shooting" Codi, and it opened the doors to what is now a lifestyle of learning. Attending the Karen Pryor Academy was one of the most challenging and exciting learning experiences in my dog-training career. Thanks to those who worked to put that program together to better the skills and the knowledge base of trainers across the world.

Introduction to Part 1

"No problem can be solved within the same consciousness which created it." Albert Einstein

The dogs are all different, but the nervous laughter coupled with the strain I see on the faces of people is similar each time I walk into a home and hear, "My dog is out of control," or "My dog never listens to me." Most of the disgruntled pet parents I encounter had imagined something quite different in terms of life with their dog; something much more relaxed and peaceful. Fortunately, when owners are willing to work on these problems, I have seen their hopes fulfilled—and that is the reason for this book.

Working with wild and unruly canines is the focus of my training, my livelihood. I interact nearly every day with people who are having difficulty getting their dogs to calm down, relax, and be more enjoyable companions. These are not usually neglected or abused dogs, and it is not as if the dogs are always devoid of basic skills, such as the ability to sit or lie down when asked. But even while performing these behaviors, they often display a deeper problem, a level of unfocused energy or wildness that negatively impacts the relationship between these dogs and their humans. Consequently, teaching basic skills is not a big part of my private training business. Rather, I instruct pet parents how to understand and teach their dogs exercises that allow them to calm down, focus, and relax. That is the mainstay of what I instruct and the heart of this book.

Part 1 will help you identify and clarify what causes your wild and crazy dog to behave the way he does. First you will learn there are a number of factors that play a part in a dog's unruly or unfocused behaviors, and in some cases, high levels of stress. Then we will broadly review the types of training methods and techniques that work best for dealing with these kinds of behaviors. This will give you a solid foundation of knowledge before you actually start training the exercises in Part 2 that will address your dog's particular problems.

As you take this journey, both you and your dog will achieve a more relaxed state of mind and body, and you will develop an improved relationship with that ideal dog you always wanted—the one who was there all along.

Chapter 1

Why Can't My Dog Relax?

Oh those wild and crazy dogs and puppies! How we love the energy but hate the repercussions of all that arousal! Mouthing, tugging on clothes, biting the leash, chewing everything in sight, and good old-fashioned body slamming akin to World Wrestling Entertainment are some of the more common complaints brought to behavior consultants and trainers all over the country as pet parents seek help for their "out of control" dogs.

Living with a dog who is unmanageable, nearly impossible to keep calm, or who seldom slows down is not only challenging and difficult, but many people believe there is no way the dog will ever learn to relax. This is especially true when the dog in question lacks impulse control, is seemingly hyperactive, or resorts to aggression when he is revved up. Even with the best of intentions, poor training or management techniques may actually make some of these antsy dogs even worse. Regardless of the reasons for the wild behaviors, one thing is clear: These are very common problems resulting in that very common question—"What is going on?"

Factors Underlying Wild and Crazy Behaviors

The answer is that there are many underlying factors at work that result in such behaviors. Some factors are based on genetics and some are environmental. Some are the result of human intervention (both good and bad), and some are the result of early interactions (or lack thereof) with littermates and other dogs. Some factors are inter-related and some act independently.

While most of the resulting "hyper" or wild behaviors can be toned down with a better understanding of dog behavior, proper training, and behavior modification, there may be medical conditions involved that require veterinary intervention. If you have a dog who cannot be calmed through the types of training and exercises included in this book, you should take him to a vet to see if there are underlying medical reasons for his behavior.

Here are the factors that I have found frequently contribute to dogs displaying out of control behaviors:

- Breed differences

- Lack of or poor early socialization

- "Solo" dogs, dogs without littermates

- Poor training methods

- Misuse of training equipment

- Exercise—too much or not enough

- Rest and sleep factors

- Lack of mental stimulation

- Touching and handling—too much or not enough

- Lack of respect for a dog's boundaries

- Sudden changes (additions/subtractions) in a dog's life

- Negative experiences

- Diet

- Social pressures from humans

It's not hard to imagine how a dog who is characterized by one or more of the above factors may have difficulty exhibiting calm behaviors. A dog who is bred to be intensely reactive to his surroundings, does not receive adequate exercise, and never learned as a puppy to be comfortable around strangers has three major strikes against him. By contrast, a well-socialized dog bred to be a companion to humans who gets moderate amounts of exercise—everything else being equal—should be much more relaxed and calm. If you take the time to profile your own dog by reading through each of the following factors, you can then begin to shape his training and daily habits to help develop a more calm and relaxed dog. As you read the following sections, see if you can pinpoint some of the areas that may be driving up your dog's activity level.

Breed Differences

Dog breeds have evolved out of our human desire to mold certain physical attributes, temperament, or looks in the dogs we raise. However, there are often less than positive ramifications from this process. For example, dogs who are bred specifically for hunting, herding, or working are often off the charts with energy and can be hyper-focused toward achieving certain goals. They are constantly thinking things like "I must catch that rat" or "herd those sheep." Dogs like these can be very compulsive and vigorous toward meeting those ends, especially if these needs are unfulfilled during their daily activities and interactions with people. "Catch that rat" becomes "catch anything that moves" and "herd those sheep" becomes "herd those children." Companion dogs, on the other hand, are likely to be much less energetic and reactive, and content to sit on the couch with you for hours.

Some breeds are just naturally energetic.

5

While I don't want to stereotype any breed, most dog trainers will tell you that a high percentage of "wild and crazy" dogs come from the Herding (think Border Collie), Working (think Labrador Retriever), and Terrier (pick one!) groups. These types of breeds can be fun and exciting to live with, but often require a lot of forethought to achieve the balance of mental and physical exercise necessary to satisfy both areas of activity and to keep energy levels down to maintain temperaments at manageable levels.

Early Socialization Factors

For dogs, the challenge of living in our world begins early in life. During the first few months of a puppy's existence, he is taking in lots of information that will help determine how he behaves in respect to other dogs, the environment around him, and toward people. This time is critical in deciding the shape and size of a puppy's brain, as well as building the fundamentals of a stable and steady temperament. Puppies without proper socialization and/or who are subjected to punishment and rough treatment in the first few months of their lives can actually suffer from deficiencies that result in poor or voided connections that would normally take place in the brain as they mature. Failure to properly expose puppies to a wide variety of experiences and stimuli often leads to fearful reactions to new situations as the dog gets older.

Sadly, proper early socialization and training are among the most neglected areas by some breeders and owners, making it difficult to raise a behaviorally sound dog. A full 96% of all dogs relinquished to shelters have had no formal training, according to a study titled "Why Do Pets End Up In Shelters?" (National Council on Pet Population Study and Policy, 1998.) The study found that there is a direct correlation between people surrendering their dogs and the lack of proper socialization and training before being given up to a shelter. In addition, most veterinarians conclude they euthanize far more dogs for behavior and aggression problems arising out of lack of socialization/training than for early puppy diseases. Many modern veterinarians, and recently the American Veterinary Society of Animal Behavior (AVSAB), have issued statements about the importance of early socialization versus the minuscule probability of a puppy catching a disease. (AVSAB, 2008. See References for additional information on citations.)

Proper socialization includes exposing puppies to a wide variety of people, dogs, and environments. Puppies left tucked away in their homes during the critical socialization period (the first four months) are much more likely to develop fears or suffer anxieties when exposed to novel things later in life. Fear and anxiety can manifest itself into the types of wild and unruly behavior I am focusing on in this book. Puppies should be given the freedom to explore new things (without force) until they are comfortable and at ease. For example, allowing a puppy to explore and approach a supervised and quiet child who tosses him yummy treats means the puppy may put a checkmark in the "I like children" column of his list of likes and dislikes.

Despite all the benefits of early socialization, you need to do your best to not expose puppies to negative experiences that might have a long-lasting impact. For example, if a child is allowed to handle a puppy roughly or inappropriately, it may do more harm than good and cause the puppy to dislike children altogether.

Puppies who have had good experiences with children usually grow up to be gentle and calm around kids.

In general, taking your puppy to training classes is a great way to socialize him. However, poorly supervised puppy classes that promote "free-for-alls" and permit dogs to run, jump, bite, mount, and bully one another, all in the name of socialization, can have a lasting effect on a dog's adult behavior around other dogs. These classes can inadvertently teach puppies rough play-styles, foster fear of other dogs, and allow them to become overly stimulated in the process. This type of contact and engagement not only lowers the puppy's tolerance of many every day things such as ease of handling, but also inhibits the puppy's ability to calm down afterward. This can be equated to kids spending all day at an amusement park and then are unable to sleep because they are so wound up and cranky from all the excitement.

Even with the support and approval of modern veterinarians for early socialization, you should still be aware of the risks of exposing an under-vaccinated puppy to environments where he might contract a disease. Letting your puppy play with unknown dogs or letting him loose in a poorly maintained or unsupervised dog park could result in health problems.

Did You Know?

The ideal puppy class teaches puppies to focus primarily on their owners. It is the owner who allows the dog to interact with the other puppies. And all of the puppies are required to "check in" with their owners frequently. Puppies attending this type of class are inoculated, in a sense, from future fears and terrors, and learn to be steady in many settings. They also learn to quietly interact with their human companions, even when there are other dogs around.

The take-home message is the importance of early puppy socialization and proper exposure to life's surprises and challenges so that puppies can grow into happy and secure adult dogs.

Solo Puppies

If the responsibly of properly raising a puppy is not enough, those who take on "Solo" puppies face an even more difficult task. Solo puppies are those that are the only puppy in a litter, or a single puppy removed early on from its litter and raised alone. Puppies learn much of their doggie social skills, including bite inhibition, from their mothers and littermates. Devoid of parental guidance or sibling input, "Solo" puppies often have lower thresholds for stimulation and often respond inappropriately toward other dogs and people.

Impact of Dog Training Methods

Adding to the complexity of two very different species living under the same roof are varied opinions about how to train dogs. There are almost as many dog training styles as there are dogs, but most progressive dog trainers today agree that positive, reward-based training works best in general, and especially when solving problem behaviors. A study published in the February 2004 issue of the *British Journal of Animal Welfare* found that: "rewards were more effective in eliciting desired behaviors from dogs...." The same study also found that "...those owners who used punishment-based training had seen a variety of bad behaviors in their dogs including barking at/aggression towards people and other dogs, fearfulness, excitement, separation anxiety, and inappropriate mounting." The authors of the study also state that "The use of punishment-based training might create a state of anxiety or conflict in the dog that is later expressed as bad behavior." Dogs who were trained exclusively using positive, rewards-based training were found to be significantly more obedient than those trained using punishment and force.

A more recent training trend, popularized on TV, recommends owners should exhibit more "leadership" towards their dogs. Leadership *should* be defined as the ability to guide, direct, or influence—and that is indeed the proper way to view an owner's relationship with a dog. Unfortunately, some owners take being a leader to mean they should dominate and intimidate their dogs to enforce behaviors. In my work experience with people and their dogs, I find the definition of leadership has become skewed and so twisted out of shape that a contortionist would be hard pressed to keep up. These misshapen ideas leave many pet parents confused—and if *they* are confused, just think how the dogs must feel with so many conflicting messages, all in the name of training!

You may have heard from friends or family members how to train your dog and how fast some methods "fix" the problems of misbehaving, anxious, and impulsive dogs. However, fast is not necessarily a fix, nor does it create an internal calmness within your dog, especially when many of those quick methods use punishment, intimidation, and fear to accomplish the results. Be wary of quick fixes!

Positive training, on the other hand, does not mean you have to be indulgent. To help your dog understand and learn, you will need to teach and guide him until he is able to do the things you want. And you will continue to teach him until he can do them reliably. Until that time, you should supervise and help him make good decisions using methods of training that promote a strong relationship of trust, not fear. This is not much different from raising well-rounded children.

However, even when people use proper and humane training techniques, many do not manage their dogs or enforce rules in a consistent fashion. For example, sometimes it is OK for the dog to get on the bed, sometimes it's not. For many dogs, what would be *really* useful is a book for dogs, titled, "The How to Live with Humans Manual" as we seem to be "malfunctioning" all the time, at least from the dog's perspective. It would be helpful if our dogs could turn to the chapter on "Things that REALLY annoy humans" to learn that we don't like them to jump all over our guests, steal food off the counter, or chew the kids' shoes. Alternately, maybe the dog could look up, "How to get humans to play ball, especially when they are busy in the bathroom," which is every ball-crazy dog's first priority. Life would be so much easier for our dogs and us with such a book.

Since we don't have that manual to share with our canine friends, it is important to keep in mind that humans and dogs are two very different species and that alone can put them at odds with one another. This is frequently due to our differing forms of communication. It is often tricky for humans to understand the "language" of canines, and vice-versa. This can create anxiety for both species when no one is able to get their message across.

The good news is, as you read the following sections, you *will* be able to interpret your dog's "language," as well as communicate more clearly with him in a way he will understand. That, along with the training exercises in Part 2 of this book, will give you a better understanding about what makes Fido tick and you will intrinsically ease your dog's day-to-day stressors and use this knowledge to help him live a calmer life. This is the core foundation to good training and leadership.

Impact of Dog Training Equipment

In addition to the problem of differing training methods, the use of harsh training equipment such as choke chains, pinch collars, and electronic shock collars can cause undue stress and anxiety and may lead to fear and aggression. This can happen when a dog is "popped, pinched, or shocked" in the presence of another dog or people. These "corrections" are often done when a dog is showing normal canine responses like excitement or fear. Many dogs quickly make the association that every time he sees things such as other dogs or kids on skateboards, it brings about a painful pull on a choke chain, so other dogs or kids on skateboards must not be safe, and therefore, reactive behaviors often increase.

Choke chains and other punitive methods of training are designed to punish unwanted behaviors but do not teach correct behavior. In many cases will actually "shut down" your dog. These punishers can frighten and eventually dampen a dog's personality so that they dread making a mistake and being corrected. It's no wonder that most people report that when they take the choke chains and pinch collars off, the dog no longer responds.

The very names of the different devices say it all—choke chains, pinch collars, and electronic shock collars—they are designed to punish and cause pain and have no place in modern, stress-free training.

Exercise—Too Little or Too Much

It is understandable that most breeds of dogs left alone all day in a house need to be exercised, be it a brisk walk around the block or a fun game of chase or retrieve. This is especially true if you have a breed that tends towards higher natural energy levels. If you do not provide your dog with the proper amount of exercise you will indeed have problems if your goal is a calm and relaxed dog.

On the other hand, your dog may actually need less exercise than you think. Observations and field studies of dogs living in the wild or in third world villages conclude that these dogs often "exercise" much less than most people would imagine. In the book *Dogs, A New Understanding,* by Raymond and Lorna Coppinger, the authors observed that the main physical exercise village dogs get is simply placing themselves near where food "shows up," principally refuse sites. (Coppinger, 2001.)

When considering the amount of exercise a dog needs, one of the first considerations should be the ability to dissipate heat. Unlike humans with all of our sweat pores and exposed skin, dogs are covered with fur and therefore have a less efficient means of overall cooling than we do. The tongue, nose, and the pads of a dog's feet are their main heat outlets, but the pads provide very little surface for good cooling. It stands to reason that larger (over 50 pounds) and heavily furred dogs have greater difficulty cooling their bodies, especially in areas where the weather is warmer, and consequently, should not be encouraged to exercise as much as smaller dogs with less fur (for example, a Newfoundand versus a Whippet).

With a few notable exceptions like specifically-bred dogs that are designed and trained for long distance, most dogs are sprinters, designed to move quickly for short distances and able to do so because they use liver glycogen as fuel to travel these short expanses. According to Coppinger, this fuel can be used up in less than a minute, and then the body must switch to burning fatty acids to continue past that level. If you think about it, dogs in the wild are at a disadvantage if they are burning precious reserves of energy beyond what is needed for survival and safety and to avoid injury. You can see how it wouldn't serve these dogs to run, play, or fight as much as we often see in our companion dogs. The dog that shares your home is still a canine with many of the same natural drives as their untamed counterparts, and it is those genetic components that hold the answers to how much exercise is really needed. In a piece from VeterinaryPartner.com, Kathy Diamond Davis says, "As in most other things, moderation works admirably for dogs when it comes to exercise. Dogs use body language to communicate and many dogs will get enough exercise just from spending interesting days with people and other animals they enjoy. Exercise that is healthy for both mind and body is the very best kind of exercise."

Did You Know?

Many experts are now saying "balance" is the key to keeping your dog in good physical condition. It is important to avoid overtaxing his body with high excitement and overly aroused states such as those seen during hard play or extensive exercise. These intense states can force dogs into an overactive stress response. This may be why many trainers and behaviorists are seeing dogs who get colossal amounts of exercise but are still unruly.

Play and high-arousal activities such as dog sports, intense ball or disc playing, over the top tug-o-war or chase games are often used as a means to exercise dogs. When trained correctly, these can be wonderful outlets for dogs with lots of energy, but the unfortunate flipside finds many dogs out of control once the play becomes too intense or lasts too long. Overtaxing your dog, either physically or mentally, can lead to severe levels of exhaustion or over-stimulation. This can then produce more roughness and cause general disquiet if he has not been taught how to stop playing and/or calm down after a rousing session of activity. There are some great books that address using play for bonding as well as for physical and mental outlets, and they are referenced in the Resources section.

Lucy and River play hard, but are both able to take breaks and rest.

Physical exercise is necessary for canine health, just as it is for us. However, your dog should be conditioned for the level of exercise you are asking of him. It is essential to consider the level of exercise your dog gets on a daily basis. Taking your dog for an infrequent run, playing a rare game of fetch, or visiting a dog park only occasionally can easily stress his body. Stay within your dog's normal limits, and keep in mind that physical exercise is only a small step on the pathway to a calm and relaxed dog.

Rest and Sleep Factors

Martina Scholz and Clarissa von Reinhardt, authors of the book *Stress in Dogs*, have found that many dogs are living with erratic sleep cycles in near states of exhaustion. Simply stated, they are not getting enough rest and sleep. The most stable dogs are found to rest and sleep seventeen or more hours per day, something that is not always possible for dogs living in busy, active homes.

If your household is continually buzzing with activity, which might be the case in homes with small children or several energetic dogs, your dog may not be getting enough rest. It's important that you provide your dog with plenty of quiet and "down" time so he is able to recuperate from play, training, or just being in the middle of life's activities.

Take note of the amount of rest and sleep your dog is getting each day and if it's less than 17 hours, consider making changes that will facilitate better rest for him. Crates and quiet rooms away from the everyday traffic of busy households make for good resting places.

Did You Know?

Dogs that spend most or all of their lives in yards can fall into sleep-deprivation cycles, since they tend to live with constant stimulation of sounds, sights, and smells from the regular activity in neighborhoods or from wildlife. These dogs are usually more stressed and are at risk for more behavior problems, including jumping, barking, digging, and aggression.

Your dog should be given lots of opportunities to sleep throughout the day.

Lack of Mental Stimulation

As with physical exercise, it is interesting to consider how dogs live (and lived) in the wild and the mental stimulation they receive. While these dogs may not be constantly on the move, they exert a lot of mental energy searching for food and monitoring their environment. Even though your dog lives in the comfort of your home, he still has an inborn or innate drive for mental stimulation, especially as it relates to acquiring food.

Many owners do not take advantage of this opportunity. When you put your dog's daily food ration in a bowl a couple of times each day and it's gone in 30 seconds or less, your dog no longer has a job to look forward to for the remainder of his day, especially if his drive for food is strong or his energy level is high. This drive can rear its ugly head with destructive behaviors such as digging, barking, or chewing, all of which help to relieve the stress created by lack of mental stimulation.

An easy way to augment your dog's mental exercise needs is to train him using food rewards. Training is a great outlet and using food helps satisfy that need to search and find the next meal. There are also many products available to keep the minds of dogs challenged and well exercised. Kongs™, Buster Cubes™, and many spin-off products are available to make each meal a mental challenge for your dog. This will help satisfy his natural drive to find food. Even something as simple as chewing raw bones or rawhides can provide a great mental and physical workout since chewing relieves stress, takes a certain amount of physical strength, and has a wonderful mental component for most dogs. (Be sure to consider your dog's chewing style before leaving him alone unsupervised with recreational chewing items.)

Heidi gets mental stimulation chewing on a Kong.

My experience working with dogs and their owners has shown me that keeping a balance between mental and physical exercise is the key to getting a dog's impulses under control. By adding more mental stimulation and keeping physical exercise to a conditioning level (ten to twenty minutes twice a day, depending on size and age of the dog), many pet parents are finding more relaxed and contented dogs. (See "Thirty Quick Tips," on page 180 for ideas on mental stimulation.)

Touching and Handling

The research is in. Dogs exposed to rough or harsh handling, such as body pounding, fast patting, or ruffling up of fur, can suffer many types of health and behavioral concerns, making them more susceptible to chronic illness and stress-related problems. While the amount of rough handling a dog can tolerate (and *tolerate* is the operative word) will vary from breed to breed, it can be a factor in increasing a dog's level of reactivity and unsteadiness.

Additionally, preliminary findings in a study by the College of Veterinary Medicine at the University of Missouri showed positive changes in the production of "good chemicals" such as serotonin, beta-endorphins, and dopamine when dogs receive gentle, massage-like touching. In their studies on the effect of human touch on dogs, researchers Rebecca Johnson and Richard Meadows also found touching decreased levels in the stress hormone cortisol. This was accomplished with soft touches and gentle stroking.

Gentle, healthy touching pays off in other ways as well. Biofeedback and other brain wave tests have shown that gentle touching can heighten the brain wave patterns associated with learning and logical thinking. This means that dogs are able to learn with greater portions of brain function necessary when they receive this beneficial handling and touching. In other words, they become smarter dogs!

Respecting Your Dog's Boundaries

Imagine you have climbed into bed with a good book, a cup of hot chocolate, and just got comfortable under the covers. Suddenly several family members parade into your room every few minutes to ask you a question or request you do something for them. It would be hard to relax and enjoy your reading time alone and you might even feel angry for being subjected to such rude treatment.

Now imagine your dog has settled into his favorite spot, ready to relax his body after a hard day of being a dog. Everyone who walks by pats him, kisses him, or gives him a brisk belly rub because he looks so cute. There is not much difference between these two scenarios. It is easy to see how constantly disrupting your dog when he is resting might be just as disconcerting for him as the disruption of your reading time is for you.

Since most people expect their dogs to respect their space and boundaries, it's only fair that people do the same in return. If your dog has just settled down to rest by your feet, don't view it as an open invitation to reach down and touch him, kiss him or ruffle up his fur. In fact, this can quickly teach him never to relax in your presence.

The old adage of "Let sleeping (and resting) dogs lie," is one to live by if you want your dog to learn to relax in your presence.

Did You Know?

You can ask your dog how he feels about being touched. Rather than "having your way" with your dog, you can show him the boundary respect he deserves by using an "ask and release" system. Anytime you would like to touch or pet your dog, "ask" first by reaching out and touching him for a couple of seconds, and then "release" by moving your hand away. Once you have done that, watch his reactions after being touched—did he get wild and escalate his behavior, possibly whining, pawing, jumping, or nipping at you? Did he leave, duck, lick his mouth or turn his head, or come in closer, and relax as if he really enjoyed it? These different responses are your dog's way of telling you if he would like to be touched again or not.

Don't be offended if your dog doesn't want to be touched when you are in the mood to have contact with him; simply consider that the time is not right, he may be overly-stimulated, he may not like where you touched him, or he may have had a hard day with too many people demanding his attention and just wants to be left alone. It's never personal, it is just information that tells you how your dog is feeling, and it's important to respect him when he communicates this information to you.

Sudden Changes

Another factor that can add to instability in a dog is sudden change within the dog's household. Changes that can and do affect your dog include a new spouse, a new baby, a new dog, moving to a new home, or the addition of another species of animal, to name a few. Sudden losses, whether human or animal, are also problematic for dogs. A departure due to death, divorce, or vacation can confuse or disrupt a dog's routine. Dogs do exhibit signs of grief, so it is important to help your dog through these periods of change by allowing him ample time to grieve or adjust. Regular routines are especially important during these types of changes. Consider ways to keep your dog's routine as normal as possible when there are any life changes in your home. Don't create even more stress on your dog by trying to rapidly increase the amount of training you do—build up gradually.

Since some changes are planned, you can make adjustments ahead of time to accommodate your dog's needs. While you can't always plan ahead for a things like a loss in the family, you can be proactive and give some thought to what you would do if something happened to change your life. Who could you call to help you? Do you have a place to take your dog if needed? Interview dog walkers and dog sitters or visit boarding kennels so you're ready if you ever need to call someone in or board your dog. That way you won't have the added guilt of turning your dog over to an unfamiliar person should there be a need. Having a plan in place before any life-changing events occur, will make a much easier transition for you and your dog.

Did You Know?

Your dog's emotional well-being will be affected to some degree whenever there are household changes, and some changes will affect your dog more than others will. Dogs often revert back to earlier puppy behaviors that received lots of attention when they were young. Many people report their dogs began chewing again or their dog had house training lapses during household changes. Your dog is not trying to add to your stress with these attention-seeking behaviors, he is simply communicating that he is also stressed.

Negative Experiences

Dog trainers talk a lot about "generalization," which is a dog's ability to learn something or perform a behavior in a variety of situations or environments. An example of an inability to generalize is when pet parents train their dog something like "sit." The dog does it very well in the house, but the minute you step out of the house together, he acts as if he never heard the word before. He has not learned to generalize the behavior. This is why trainers will instruct people to practice a behavior in many locations so their dogs are able to do it in different places and generalize the skill.

What dogs *can* and *do* generalize well, however, are things that promote their survival, such as fear and aggression. If a Golden

Retriever attacks another dog, the victim dog will likely generalize this and learn to fear and/or react to all dogs who look like Golden Retrievers. Conversely, if the attacking dog was a female, the dog who was attacked may respond negatively to all female dogs. If an attack is extremely traumatic, he may have issues with all other dogs in general. This same generalization process can also happen with a dog's relationship with humans. If a little boy falls on a dog, the dog may react poorly with all children in that age range, or just little boys, or all small humans.

These types of scars can run deep for many dogs, and are often carved deeper when these associations are not clearly identified and desensitized right away. If you find that your dog has a fear or reacts toward specific things or people, it is important to prevent exposure while working with a qualified behavior and training expert to help your dog with the problem. See Resources to find a qualified behavior and training expert.

It will be impossible to help your dog relax around the people, circumstances, or dogs that trigger negative reactions until you put your dog through an effective behavior modification and training program. If your dog is continually exposed to the very things that caused the reaction in the first place, the chances of the reaction growing stronger increase with each incident.

Diet

It is recognized by many dog professionals that diet can impact a dog's behavior. Steve Lindsay's well respected *Handbook of Applied Dog Behavior and Training* cites a number of scientific studies supporting this claim. Because this is such an important subject, I have devoted an entire chapter to it. (See Chapter 2.)

Social Pressure from Humans

Disappointment with owning a dog who is not as well behaved as "Lassie," or some previously owned dog, can add to some of the problematic behaviors in dogs. No one intends to have a "problem" dog, and pet parents often face feelings of sadness, anger, or frustration when things do not go as planned. Responding to your dog's behaviors in this way can make it difficult for your dog to relax and be calm.

Embarrassment can also keep tensions between you and your dog at a heightened level, as almost everyone cares what other people think about how their dogs behave. It's normal to take it personally when dogs act wild in public or with your guests. Unfortunately, that can also lead to isolation from friends, family, or community functions, adding to the frustration of having a dog that no one likes to be around.

It is often difficult to separate personal feelings from your dog's behavior issues when trying to figure out how to manage living with a "problem" dog. However, by doing so, you can help ease the emotions and that will then allow you to work on the problems without judging your dog unfairly or suffering from the feeling that others are judging you because of your dog.

It is important to remember that your dog does not "choose" to be wild or crazy, and that it would be much easier for him if you train him to relax and calm down. As with humans, control and predictability are what keep our stress levels in check, and it's no different for your dog. The following sections will help you understand how to help your dog in these areas.

The Role of Stress

You might ask yourself why any dog gets "stressed out," especially since, at least on the surface, it appears as though most dogs have it made. Countless canines have comfy homes, fancy beds, lots of human attention, are waited upon with bowls of gourmet dog food at designated meal times, walked, fluffed, coiffed, and pampered beyond the imagination of many humans—all making it difficult to understand what dogs might have to be stressed about.

All dogs exhibit some stress from time to time; it is natural and necessary for survival. However, when you encounter or live with a "wild and crazy" dog, he is most likely a dog with higher stress levels than calm and relaxed dogs. Greatly simplified, stress comes in two general forms: good stress, such as the exuberance your dog exhibits when you come home from work each day; and bad stress, which is brought on by panic, fear, worry, or anger due to one or more of the factors discussed above.

Our dogs seem to have it made these days. Jesse James rides in his stroller while shopping with his pet parent.

When a dog is under stress, the sympathetic nervous system releases adrenaline, cortisol, and other chemicals into the bloodstream, which then combine to push many organs of the body into high gear. This is an involuntary response that forces the heart, lungs, and blood pressure to "step on the gas," so to speak. Voilá, a "wild and crazy," as well as a stressed dog.

From an evolutionary standpoint, the kicking in of these chemicals played an important role in the survival of the species. It allowed dogs to run away faster, successfully pursue prey, put more energy into display behaviors, or have the energy to put up a grand fight if necessary. These same chemical processes still take place today with our pet dogs. For some, chemicals kick in at the sight or sound of a "scary" letter carrier, while for others, that same flood of chemicals might happen when they are confined by leashes, doors, or fences and are suddenly and highly aroused by things in their environment (such as other dogs, wildlife, or people). With no way to "work" that arousal off, many dogs resort to barking, lunging, and other intense displays. Even during play, this chemical process is taking place and can be witnessed at dog parks, dog daycares, and other dog gathering places. Anticipation and the flow of chemicals rises with each step a dog takes closer to the park or play area. Stress hormones (both good and bad responses) are literally thick around dog parks and other communal dog gathering areas.

Unfortunately, there are several downsides to this "chemical flood," especially when a dog is constantly exposed to an environment where such a flow is stimulated. The half-life of the stress hormone cortisol is about 20 minutes after an aroused state, which means it can take a full 40 minutes for complete recuperation. If stressors keep presenting on a regular basis, as is common among dogs living in shelters or crowded kennels, the dog may never reach a relatively calm state and begin to display lower tolerances for things that might not be a big deal under normal circumstances. The longer a dog is stressed, especially if it goes on for days, the worse it gets for the dog. One consequence is that stress can deplete the body of "good chemicals" that help dogs calm down and relax. These include chemicals like serotonin, dopamine, and of course, endorphins. This reduction of good chemicals can, and does, eventually create fatigue both mentally and physically, which adds further stress on the body and mind. In addition, a dog's immune system is depressed, leaving the animal more susceptible to illness and disease. This same process happens to humans!

Once you have a better picture of your dog's challenges with daily life, you can begin down a new road that will guide you and your dog toward goals that will benefit both of you and help to achieve a happier and more relaxed life together. That is why it is important to consider your dog's lifestyle, breed, and environment as a total package. It will help you identify any compounding factors that might add to discourse and to physical and/or mental stress.

Physiological Reasons for Stress

As mentioned previously, environmental stressors and psychological issues related to the factors described above can play a big part in what stresses dogs—but there are also physiological reasons that can cause stress. The list of medical reasons for stress vary from musculo-skeletal problems, diminishing of the senses due to disease, injury, aging, chronic pain, frustrated intact males, females in season, lack of proper rest or sleep, exhaustion, thyroid problems, cancer, kidney problems, obesity, cardiovascular problems, and many more.

The loss of any of the senses can also cause grave distress for some dogs, since they will feel more vulnerable and anxious as their eyesight or hearing begins to diminish, both of which can happen to younger dogs as well as those that are aging. As dogs grow older, they may appear less cooperative and more grumpy as they try to figure out how to get around and meet their needs while still remaining safe. This, of course, can be taxing and your dog may display unwanted behaviors during these transitions.

Did You Know?

It is common for dogs with chronic pain to show signs of stress. These signs can be confused with behavior symptoms, including things such as panting, red eyes, sweaty paws, chewing on oneself, and more. A trip to the veterinarian is in order if you notice any of these signs or sudden changes in behavior.

If your dog has not had a complete examination by his veterinarian recently, that is a good place to begin before assuming your dog "just has behavior problems." It is always best to eliminate medical reasons before moving to on to behavioral modification and training programs.

CHAPTER 2

HOW DIET AFFECTS BEHAVIOR IN DOGS

As has been discussed, wild and crazy behaviors in dogs can result from a number of different factors ranging from genetics to training methods to early negative experiences. In addition, they can be the result of some physiological problems. Any one or a combination of these factors could be impacting your dog.

What was not well known until recently is the role of diet. Things like excessive barking, mood swings, restless sleep, compulsive disorders, reactivity, aggression, hyperactivity, and biting can all be symptoms of a poor diet. Along with training your dog to be calmer and more relaxed, it is important to consider his diet. If his unwanted behaviors are caused by his diet, your success with training and helping him to relax may be limited. To avoid these limitations, take some time to do your homework and look at your dog's food.

You can start your investigation with a close look at nutritional models for humans. This avenue can help you to learn about food choices that negatively influence how humans behave and, as you will see, affect the way your dog behaves as well.

Did You Know?

The Child Wisdom web site (see Resources) has great information about how food affects human children. We now know that similar processes are at work with our pet dogs:

Food Sensitivities/Allergies—Some people get depressed or behave irrationally after they eat (often unknowingly) something to which they are sensitive or allergic. This phenomenon, sometimes called a "brain allergy" has been widely reported and sometimes appears in patients who display mental health symptoms. True classic food allergies involve an antigen-antibody immune response (IgE-mediated) and are relatively rare. About 5% of children and about 2% of adults are reported to have these "true food allergies." In contrast, food sensitivities, sometimes called food intolerances, are reported by almost 25% of Americans... Any food may cause a reaction, but the most commonly reported food sensitivities involve wheat gluten, dairy products, yeast, corn, eggs, soy, grapes, oranges, chocolate and synthetic food additives.

While dogs are classified as carnivores, they are known to eat both plant matter and meat. Based on many field observations, "opportunistic scavengers" has become the more fitting description of their dietary practices—eating whatever is available. It's no wonder that dogs will eat just about anything that is put in their bowls, including processed pet foods with minimal nutritional value. Just because most dogs will eat whatever is put in their bowl doesn't mean it's good for them—many of our pets are eating foods that can be linked to behavioral problems.

Feeding for Behavioral Health—What's in Your Dog's Bowl?

As pet parents and providers, it's important to give active thought to what you feed your dog since different foods will lead to different results. According to many veterinary and behavior experts, we are producing generations of health and behavior problems for dogs by feeding overly-processed, chemical and dye-laden commercial dog foods that appear wonderful to humans, but often have nutritional deficits and long-term toxic effects.

Part of this problem starts with the companies producing many of the popular name brands of food. A *Whole Dog Journal* article entitled "Made in a Secret Location," written by Nancy Kern, states:

> Mostly, the giant companies, corporate cousins to the human food manufacturing industry, serve (partially) to spin figurative gold out of the "straw" leftovers from the human food side. The human food processors use the good parts, and the food fragments that would otherwise be wasted are put to good use in pet foods. The result is a consistent, inexpensive, but not particularly healthy food that is readily available anywhere in the country.

Furthermore, consider this:

> The "whole grains" used in many dog foods have had the starch removed and the oil extracted (usually by chemical processing) for vegetable oil; or they are the hulls and other remnants from the milling process. If whole grains are used, they may have been deemed unfit for human consumption because of mold, contaminants, or poor storage practices. (Messonnier, 2000.)

An additional problem is the use of corn in commercial dog foods. Used as a protein source to save money in many popular foods, corn can reduce the amount of serotonin in a dog. "A common protein source in dog food is corn. Corn, however, is unusually low in tryptophan and represents some risk to animals sensitive to serotonergic under activity," according to canine researcher James O'Heare. Serotonin keeps dogs well-balanced and helps to control moods, arousal, and sensitivities to pain, sounds, and touch. It is also the major component in healthy sleep/wake cycles. An imbalance of serotonin can cause sleep problems which frequently exacerbate behavior problems; thus making training or modification that much more difficult. Many behaviorists and vets now recommend the complete elimination of corn in the diet because of this problem. (O'Heare, 2005.)

Other studies show that increasing the quality of food along with the levels of protein can result in calmer dogs. For example, canine behaviorist Steven Lindsay states in a recent book that researchers "... have reported that a high-quality diet with increased levels of protein (29%) and fat (20.5%) appears to produce a calming effect..." (Lindsay, 2005). We do know how junk carbohydrates and junk food affect humans, and it doesn't take much of a leap to believe that products affecting our behavior or moods can also affect dog behavior. Liz Palika, a dog trainer and writer, talks about the connection she saw in her puppy classes in an article for *Dog World Magazine*: "In 1995 and 1996 I began to notice that a number of the Labrador and Golden Retriever puppies in our puppy kindergarten classes had trouble holding still." Palika and her assistants began taking notes, talking to the owners, and recording the activity of the puppies, many of whom they concluded were "hyper." The common factor was that nearly all of the "hyper"puppies were eating a high-carb diet. Once the dogs were switched to diets that contained fewer carbohydrates, Palika noted that 75% of the puppies were noticeably calmer within two weeks. (Palika, 2002.) James O'Heare has concluded that "Much behavior is influenced by physiological processes, including the activity of the neurotransmitters and hormones. Since these chemicals are synthesized from dietary nutrients, it stands to reason that the nutrients consumed can influence the levels of some of these chemicals and the processes they are involved in." (O'Heare, 2007.)

Be an Informed Pet Parent

So what's a pet parent to do? The bags of food at pet stores and supermarkets look tantalizing, and they all claim to meet the nutritional needs of your dog. Many also claim to benefit the maintenance/health of different body types and specific groups such as large-breed puppies, overweight dogs, or senior canines. So which ones are telling the truth, and how do you choose the best possible food for your dog's needs?

The best way to understand dog food is to read the labels carefully. Dog food labels are similar to those on human food products; ingredients are listed in descending order by weight. The first five ingredients make up the bulk of the food, so those are the most important to look at when selecting a dog food brand. Meat or a specific type of meat meal should always be the first ingredient on the label. Choose a product that identifies the type of meat or meal as "chicken," or "lamb meal." Avoid those that say "poultry" or "meat meal" which can contain just about anything that fits under that title, including road kill and diseased animals.

As your investigation continues, also look to make sure the first ingredient is not a meat by-product. By-products are not muscle meats, and can include leftover animal components such as lungs, kidneys, brain, spleen, liver, bone, blood, fatty tissue, stomach, and intestines freed of their contents. There are mixed feelings about the use of by-products in dog food, but the fact is, some dogs have trouble digesting them. Given that there are many great foods that don't include by-products, it is be best to shy away from those that do.

The next step in selecting a good food is to look at the type and amounts of grains listed on the label. Grains are normally used to keep production costs down, and while certain grains are beneficial to good health, others are known to cause sensitivities. Higher grain content means you will need to feed more cups of food, since it takes a lot more grain than meat to reach the nutritional levels required to satisfy a dog's need for protein. For this reason, you can actually end up spending more per cup for many of the "cheap" brands than the high-end foods, and more frequent bowel movements could lead to house training problems or stress as your dog's need to eliminate increases. If your dog does not have free access to his potty area, he may develop anxiety problems as he tries to "hold it," to avoid having an accident in his crate or the house. Many companies now offer no-grain choices of their dog food.

In addition, carbohydrates act much like sugar. These high grain-content foods produce excessive energy for about two hours after ingestion, which is illustrated in the way athletes "carb up" for an energy boost before they need to perform. The high-carbohydrate dog foods do the same thing to your dog, except most people do not provide their canines with the right combination of mental and physical exercise necessary to work off all that energy. This can result in destruction to your home or yard, or rough play and biting.

Behaviorally speaking, everything from housetraining problems to overly energetic dogs can be linked to poor quality foods, and some of these behaviors are caused by the preservatives, additives, and dyes used in kibble. The health considerations of these compounds are plentiful and can lead to a dog displaying his distress. The chemicals most often associated with cancer and other toxic-driven diseases are the preservatives found in many dog foods. BHA (Butylated hydroxyanisole), BHT (Butylated hydroxytoluene), and Ethoxyquin are all known carcinogens and, by regulation, are limited in human food, but are used as preservatives in many dog foods and dog treats. If you see these ingredients listed on the bag, put it back on the shelf and keep looking.

It is far better to look for a food that uses natural ingredients as preservatives. Some natural alternatives are composed of tocopherols (vitamin E), citric or ascorbic acid (vitamin C), or a combination of the two. In addition, look for bag that have manufacturing dates on them, as this ensures freshness, since food preserved with products that are more natural will not have as long of a shelf life.

Those foods designed for specific age, weight, or body-types also seem like a wonderful idea. However, manufacturers simply add more supplements (that have been processed and preserved along with the food) in order to make their specialty claims. It is far better to add your own supplements with recommendations from your veterinarian or health-care advisor, but most of the high-end foods will provide all the vitamins and minerals all dogs need to maintain health.

How and When to Feed Your Dog

The ideal regimen is to feed an adult dog two or three times a day. For dogs, as with humans, energy comes from the breakdown of food into glucose, so it is important to feed regularly to prevent blood sugar levels from becoming erratic. At the other end of the feeding spectrum is leaving food out all day—so-called "free feeding." This gives your dog an abundance of energy but, if the owner is away for long periods of time, no way to expend it. When you do feed your dog, put his bowl down for no more than fifteen minutes and if he hasn't licked it clean, assume he is not hungry and pick it up until the next scheduled feeding.

As a bonus for your dog, try feeding him using food-carrier toys such as Kongs™ or Buster Cubes™ as a way to provide mental and physical exercise. These are great for those dogs that like to take their time eating. These "food puzzles" will also help slow down dogs that "vacuum" their food from the bowl at break-neck speed.

Whether it is dry kibble, canned, raw, cooked, freeze-dried, or a combination, it is essential to do your homework when choosing food for your dog. The bottom line is to read the ingredients and feed your dog healthy foods to achieve good mental and physical health for the duration of his life, as well as to help him relax from the inside while working on the outside behavioral skills.

Chapter 3

THE ROAD TO HELPING YOUR DOG RELAX

In order to achieve your goal of having a more relaxed dog, it is helpful to have a picture in your mind of what a calm, relaxed, and attentive dog looks like, how he behaves both emotionally and physically, and what he looks like when playing. Looking at both the emotional and physical components of a relaxed dog will help you to identify where your own dog fits on the continuum. And, if your dog does not look like the following portrait, don't despair, this book will help you teach your dog to relax.

Profile of a Calm Dog

An emotionally relaxed dog remains attentive, but generally does not get alarmed when things are going on around him. He may be curious about his surroundings, but not reactionary or even willing to put much effort into exploring when things change in his environment. The relaxed dog may casually explore a sound or people flowing in and around the house during normal, daily routines, but will readily go back to what he was doing after he investigates. The relaxed dog is able to accept life as it happens and does not pester or beg for things like attention or food—rather, he is laid-back and casual.

Overall, the emotionally relaxed dog will not show signs of worry, anxiety, or fear—just mild curiosity concerning his surroundings.

Many dogs may show some excitement when there are changes in their environment, such as going for a walk or being outside, but a dog with the ability to relax will recover from exciting behaviors quickly, and without continual prompting from humans.

The physical appearance of a calm dog includes one whose eyes are relaxed and often partially closed. He has a relaxed jaw. When he is moving about his mouth is slightly open, or gently closed. His breathing is quiet and soft. The tail of a relaxed dog is carried approximately even or slightly lower than his back and wags in a slow, swishy motion. For dogs whose tails naturally curl up and over their backs, the wag should also be slow, not frenzied. Interestingly enough, recent studies on tail wagging by a team of researchers from the University of Trieste and University of Bari in Italy reported that happy, relaxed dogs wag with a bias to the right side of their body. Those who are less comfortable or stressed, wag their tails with a bias to the left. (Sandra Blakeslee, 2007.)

A calm and relaxed dog.

When a relaxed dog is sitting or lying down, he will often shift his weight to one hip, and his head will be more or less even with the rest of his body, or slightly lowered, rather than lifted up. When lying down, relaxed dogs will often place their head on their legs or the floor if they are lying on their chest, or they might choose to lie completely on their sides or backs. In addition, relaxed dogs will often tuck a foot under their bodies, or lay splayed-legged (frog-legged in the rear).

How Calm Dogs Play

Play for the relaxed dog contains a certain amount of control during the initiation, as well as the play itself. The dog offers polite behaviors such as play bowing or picking up a toy to present for play, but without any sense of obsession or overt displays of emotion. During play, the relaxed dog will play with glee and energy, but can easily give up the play when requested. The dog is able to come back into a relaxed and calm state within seconds and is able to move on to other things without displaying obsessive attention-seeking be-haviors after the play has ended.

When playing with another dog, the play style is characterized by some gentle mouthing and maintaining a relaxed tail. Calm dogs often lie down and paw or mouth one another. They may run, chase, or play tug, using gestures such as play bows and butt bumps be-tween sessions to slow things down and to help set the tone of the play. Calm dogs generally do not body slam, tackle, or take the other dog down, nor do they stand over the top of another dog in a threat-ening manner.

Austin and Goldie play politely and close to the ground.

Now that you have a better sense of how a calm dog should look and behave, you can compare your dog's behavior to get a better idea of where you are with your own dog. Be sure to take the Stress Test in the Resources section to help complete the profile of your dog's energy and stress levels.

Calm Yourself Down First

There are many simple ways to help your dog become more relaxed, but the first step is to decrease your own stress! It is important to lead by example as dogs can pick up on the fact that you are stressed.

Dogs communicate with each other in many different ways, including body language, marking behaviors, vocalizations, and the rhythm of their breathing. Fast, short breaths with an open mouth can indicate that your dog is on the verge of play or in an excited state. Tight, closed-mouthed, shallow, quick breaths through the nose, and/or puffing at the mouth are signs of stress and anxiety. Your dog will get the message loud and clear when you hold your breath (or are taking shallow, anxious breaths around him) that "something must be wrong!"

Breathing deeply around your dog and allowing him to hear you inhale and exhale is very calming for both of you. Even if he just ate your favorite pillow, the solution calls for calmness—respond, don't react! As difficult as it may be, it is far better to take several deep breaths and do some goal setting to prevent these situations in the first place. Reactions to unwanted behaviors often make the behavior stronger since your dog learns he will get attention for it, or it may frighten him enough that he learns to hide from you after he tears up your pillows. Dogs do not do these things to upset the humans in their lives; they do them because it is fun, relieves stress, or gets attention. You will learn more about this later, but the main point here is to lead by example—calmness begets calmness.

Understanding the Natural Behaviors Your Dog Uses to Calm Down

You can help your dog travel the road to relaxation by understanding the language that dogs comprehend best—body language and physical displays. After you learn some of the more common signals that dogs use, you will have better insight to help you understand your dog's emotional state.

Turid Rugaas, a Norwegian dog trainer and behavior expert, has studied the physical behaviors of dogs and their body language for many years. In her book *On Talking Terms with Dogs*, she coined the term "Calming Signals" when referring to behaviors that dogs display to communicate their emotional state of mind. Dogs use these behaviors with other dogs, as well as with humans, to relay their emotions and calm themselves. (Rugaas, 2006.)

Unfortunately, most people do not understand what a dog is trying to communicate, even when it is loud and clear in the dog's mind. These types of miscommunications are yet another factor that adds to the angst of our domestic dogs. It's no wonder that the family dog feels that "Nobody understands me," and it is this very lack of predictability from humans, coupled with the loss of control (due to things like barriers, leashes, fences, etc.), that become major stress issues. In addition, training tools, such as leashes, that keep your dog safe and compliant with local laws, are the same tools that regularly prevent him from doing natural calming behaviors that would actually help him resolve conflicts and relax when he is anxious and out in public.

This is why it is important to read the signals and displays that dogs use to de-escalate potential clashes and over-reactive responses. As you get better at recognizing these signals and behaviors, you will open the door to understanding more about the canine mind. In turn, this will open communication between you and your dog. By recognizing the most universal of these calming behaviors, you will be able to help your dog before his anxiety spirals into impulsive or destructive behaviors.

The good news is that it is not hard to learn the most widely used signals because they are obvious if you know what to look for. The most frequently used "calming behaviors" are the following:

- Tongue licking (the quick flicks of the tongue outside of the mouth—like licking lips)

- Sniffing the ground

- Scratching like they have fleas (when they don't have fleas)

- Shaking like a wet dog when they are not wet

- Yawning—wide, sometimes shaky yawns
- Multiple eye blinks
- Averting eyes—not making direct eye contact
- Doing something else—in effect, ignoring you
- Turning, or walking away

Tongue licking, sniffing the ground, and yawning are all calming behaviors that you should learn to recognize.

Once you become good at seeing which calming behaviors your dog uses most frequently, you may ask, "When do I know if my dog is really doing the behavior for 'legitimate reasons' and is not feeling uncomfortable or stressed?" The answer is: when the behavior makes sense in the context of the situation. In other words, if your dog shakes as if he just got out of a bath when someone pats his head, that behavior is out of context. Your dog is likely uncomfortable with this and trying to come to terms with someone touching his head.

Another way to tell is if your dog, all of a sudden, starts doing something other than what he was doing the moment before. This is often a good indicator that he is engaging in a calming behavior. Many owners I work with report their dog is unable to perform a trained behavior that "he does all the time at home," but when taken out, all he does is sniff the ground. This is usually the dog's way of trying to relax and process environmental stimuli, and another good indicator that he needs some additional direction, training, or guidance from you.

To assist your dog further, you can "mirror" many of these calming behaviors back to him. This often helps dogs calm down and relax. For example, try yawning (let your dog see your open mouth) several times when he seems anxious. It usually will not take long before you see him start to relax, and he may yawn back. You can also lick your lips while averting your eyes, or just turn your head away, which can relieve some of the pressure from feeling as though he needs to interact with you. Resist making eye contact with your dog if he is already feeling the consequences of stress.

Taking deep, audible breaths is another good way to help your dog relax. The real trick is to detach yourself when you do mirror any of these behaviors. In other words, do not make eye contact, talk to your dog, or touch him if you are trying to get him to calm down. Engaging with your dog is often exciting from his point of view, or it can make him believe he is obligated to interact with you when all he really needs is a few minutes to resolve what has him worried or excited.

If you have ever heard yourself say, "My dog is stubborn. He *knows* how to sit (come, heel, etc.), but he won't do it if we go anywhere outside the house," then your dog is likely trying to tell you something. He is not stubborn—he might be nervous, fearful, overly excited, or the behavior has not been trained in different environments—but certainly not stubborn. The same goes for behaviors like reactivity toward other dogs or humans—your dog is trying to express how he feels about the situation. Whatever the reasons, your dog is communicating that he needs some help, not criticism. Keep watching for those calming signals that will give you insight into what might be going on so you can help your dog process a situation before he feels the need to take things up a notch.

As the title of this book implies, you can actually teach your dog how to relax himself and successfully calm down after he's become excited and/or is showing the effects of stress. This is accomplished with a variety of simple exercises that not only reinforce him for calm behaviors, but also teach him new skills to settle himself down. If you want to get the maximum out of using this book, start with a simple recipe for success: To encourage calmness, reward it whenever you see it.

Rewarding Calm Behaviors

Dogs continually offer calm behaviors, but unfortunately, they are often ignored (this happens to children also)! This can lead them to believe that calm behaviors are not worth much. Dogs can and do learn calm behaviors as quickly as they learn the wild and unwanted ones, so show your dog what you would like him to do by rewarding the behaviors you like. You can simply smile and say, "Good dog," in a quiet voice, or you can walk by and drop a treat at his feet, or you can do a combination of both. (Get in the habit of carrying a few treats with you, or have treats stashed around the house so you don't miss opportunities to reward your dog.)

When you use praise to acknowledge your dog's calmness, make sure your voice is calm and soft, say it only once, and resist making eye contact so your dog will not feel obligated to engage. This will really help him get the message that all he has to do to get your attention or a food reward is kick back and relax! Since dogs are opportunists, this will be a simple task.

CHAPTER 4

ESSENTIAL TRAINING CONCEPTS

There are many great books currently on the market on how to train and manage dogs using positive concepts. The purpose of this chapter is to provide an overview of these modern methods of dog training which I believe are imperative to use when dealing with excited and/or unruly dogs. You will need to understand these concepts before moving on to Part 2 of this book where specific training exercises to promote calmness and relaxation are presented. If you are not already familiar with positive training methods, you should take the time to read over the material in this chapter and check out the recommended reading list in the Resources at the back of the book.

Realize that Dogs are Dogs

When people begin a journey with a dog, one of the most important things they need to realize is that dogs walk along a different path than they do. The way dogs do things does not always conform to what we humans prefer in terms of our own comfort and pleasure. Dogs are best at being dogs—they are not born understanding human rules. The key is to reward dogs in such a way that they will do things that are more compatible with how you live your life—but also allow them the freedom to enjoy just being a dog.

Dogs are good "accountants." They use a cost-benefit analysis approach to just about anything. When told to do something, the dog asks himself "What's in it for me?" This is the process dogs go through as they consider how to respond to the requests of humans. With that in mind, each time you respond to your dog's behavior, it provides him with instant feedback about whether he should choose that behavior again or not—what is the cost and what is the benefit? If you provide a benefit, it is more likely your dog will do the behavior again. If not, he won't. You are constantly training your dog whether you realize it or not.

This dog is weighing the benefits of maintaining a sit versus going after a favorite toy.

Positive Training to Relax Your Dog

Positive reinforcement training teaches your dog that when he does a behavior correctly, he will be rewarded for his efforts, much like the way you get a paycheck for doing your job. While positive reinforcement can be used to achieve all sorts of amazing behaviors, with wild and crazy dogs we are going to focus on rewarding calm and relaxed behaviors.

Reward or reinforcement training is a very successful method with a strong scientific background supporting its long-term benefits. It is also a just and humane way of communicating to your dog what you would like him to do. The results of this style of training are easily seen as your dog is rewarded for his cooperation, and, as a bonus, your relationship is strengthened. Simply put, positive reinforcement training allows dogs to be enthusiastic about experimenting and discovering what they need to do to make the good things happen—in this case, relaxing!

Using Markers

Positive reinforcement training allows you to exploit the accountant in your dog by teaching him that if he does what you ask, he will get what he wants—food, toys, walks, petting, play, or anything else that matters to him. However, he has to know what he did right so he will be able to repeat it. In other words, you need a means by which to tell your dog when he gets the correct answer. The way to accomplish this is by using a marker signal to let him know when he is correct—otherwise he won't understand what you want from him.

Most dog trainers today recommend using a clicker to mark behavior. The clicker is a small mechanical device that, when pushed, makes a clicking sound. You click as your dog is doing the behavior you want. Clicking is always followed up with some sort of reward—usually food. Timing is very important so the dog knows exactly what he did to earn the reward. If you want to explore clicker training in more detail, there are many good books and DVDs available on the subject in the Resources.

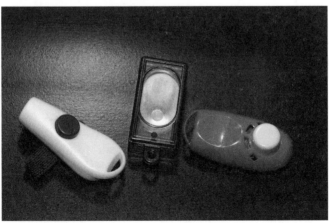

Different types of clickers.

Clickers make the best marker signals since the crisp, sharp sound they make is an effective way to mark or capture a precise moment in time. It is important for your dog's success that he has a very clear way to know what he did to earn the reward that follows the marker signal. However, not everyone can have a clicker at hand all the time, and some people find them difficult to use. Verbal markers such as "Good boy," are an alternative, but they can be too slow when you are trying to be precise. If you choose not to use a clicker, use a short, sharp word like, "Yip." It is quick and fun to say, and not used as much in our daily interactions with dogs. If using a verbal marker, try to say it with the same speed and tone each time so your dog doesn't become confused by the different voice pitches and connotations of speech.

Rules for Using Marker Signals

Whether using a clicker or a marker word, it is important that you play "by the rules," so your dog can truly understand what you want from him.

The first rule for marking a behavior is to click or say your marker word just as the behavior is being done, and then quickly follow with a food reward. It's important to do both so that the dog knows the mark means a reward is coming. Even if you marked at the wrong time, you still must reward your dog. If you don't, your dog will not always believe that a reward is coming, and may choose to do something else that he finds more interesting or fun.

Another rule when using a marker signal is to only use it one time, even if your dog did something spectacular. Otherwise you are likely to make it unclear which behavior you want to reinforce.

Try to avoid showing your dog the reward until after using the marker signal. The idea is that he will learn to offer behaviors, hoping he can get you to click or use your marker word. If he sees the reward, he may stop thinking about the behavior and get distracted by the sight of the food or toy or whatever you are using that he finds rewarding. If you are using food as a reward, buy a small treat pouch in which to put your food rewards. That can help you refrain from holding food in your hand where your dog can see it.

Bags designed to hold treats make it easier to get your rewards to your dog and help keep him from getting distracted by the sight of food.

If using a clicker, make sure the click comes first, before your other hand moves to give the reward. Many people make the mistake of using the marker signal as they are starting to give their dog the reward. That will have your dog watching your treat hand, rather than listening for the marker signal. When he responds correctly to a verbal cue such as "Sit," you should mark the behavior with a word or your clicker, and *then* give him the food. It is important that these be two separate actions so your dog learns to focus on what his body is doing and not the food in your hand. It can help to imagine that your hand is taped to your stomach or your hip, and the only way it can be moved is after the click or marker word.

This person is clicking and moving her hand with a reward toward the dog at the same time. The dog will likely only focus on the reward, not the behavior that resulted in the treat.

Once you have rewarded your dog for the correct behavior, bring your now empty treat hand up again so he doesn't learn to watch the hand with the food. This time, think of your hand as if it's attached to a bungee cord. You reach down to give your dog his reward, and then your hand is pulled back up to your waist or hip once you popped the treat into his mouth. Practice this without him present to get the timing right.

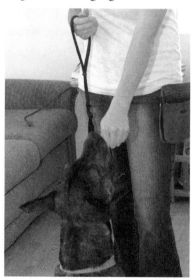

This is the correct way to mark or click and treat. First the marker signal is given, and then the reward happens.

Finally, avoid using the clicker or marker word to get your dog's attention. Since the marker tells your dog when he has the correct answer, if you click or say your marker word when your dog is ignoring you, it will tell him that ignoring is the correct answer. Teaching him to pay attention in the first place should be the focus and there are exercises in Part 2 that will help with those areas.

Let Your Marker Signal do the Talking

Allowing your clicker or marker word to do the communicating with your dog is another essential consideration as you move forward. When you are instructed to add a verbal cue during the training exercises (what is commonly called a "command"), say it only one time, then allow your dog a moment to figure it out. If you keep repeating he, your dog may learn that he should wait to hear "Sit, sit, sit," multiple times before he actually has to sit, which for him is fine since he will still get his reward. This teaches your dog to respond slowly, or to ignore the words until he feels like doing the behavior. This can also add more confusion to the process if, just as your dog was going to sit, you say, "Sit," again before he was able to finish what he had started.

The best way to communicate with your dog is to mark the correct behavior as it is in progress, which says to him, "Yes, you got the right answer, and for doing so, I'm going to give you a reward." If he does not respond within a reasonable amount of time to a verbal cue that you are sure he understands (because you have been practicing the exercises), you simply end that training session with a release cue such as, "All done." This will tell your dog he missed the opportunity for that reward, so he should pay closer attention next time you ask. If you want to give him another chance, wait a few seconds, change your position and try again.

You also need to think through what went wrong, and why your dog was unable to do the behavior. Perhaps you trained too long, he is full, he needs a drink of water, or you are asking too much of your dog and he wasn't sure what you wanted. As you work through the following training exercises, you will find sections for problem solving, so be sure to read them if your dog appears confused or is unable to do something successfully.

Food Rewards

As mentioned above, a click or other marker must be followed with a reward. A reward can be a variety of things—food, a tummy rub, a chance to chase a squirrel—but for most owners, the easiest and most effective reward is some sort of food treat. Do consider that a reward is in the eye of the beholder, so find food rewards your dog likes, not what you think he should like—as long as the ingredients are healthy.

Simply put, food equals survival for dogs, and nearly all dogs are willing to work for food. In fact, when given the choice of a "free lunch" or working for their meals, the majority of dogs choose to work. Using food during training reinforces good behaviors in two important ways. First, your dog gets to "earn" his food and satisfy his instinctive need to forage. Second, the food itself makes an impact on the brain, building and maintaining learning, which allows new behaviors to be retained longer and stronger. Once your dog understands that putting his hind end on the ground results in a tasty reward, he is likely to offer that behavior again. When you continue to "pay off" each time for sitting, he will quickly learn that sitting is a behavior that has great benefits and will offer it when he is unsure what else to do.

The fact that most dogs will work for food makes positive training easier.

When first teaching your dog any new behavior, or when beginning to work on modifying an old one, you should be generous with food rewards. If for some reason you resist using food rewards early on (as some owners do for various reasons), the dog misses building those strong neuropathways toward the new behavior. Without them, old, unwanted behaviors may be allowed to surface when he is feeling stressed or overly excited. Stress hormones and established behaviors will always trump unstable or weak behaviors, and you might find your dog pulling the old behaviors out of his toolbox when under any kind of pressure. That's why it's so important to be liberal with your food rewards in the beginning.

Early, generous use of food also enhances muscle memory. Once that happens, your dog will be able to do the behavior without thinking. He won't even have to think when he hears something like, "Sit." It will be automatic, just like many of the things you have been doing for years, such as driving a car. You don't have to think when driving your car, and many times will arrive at your destination without knowing how you got there because your muscle memory took.

People who are new to using food rewards will often ask when they can get rid of the food. It's a legitimate question since few people envision themselves carrying around a treat bag for the rest of their dog's life even though it is not much different than carrying a poop bag when you go out of the house with your dog. Others resist using food as a reward when training for any number of reasons—including their own food issues! Some are willing to try food as reinforcement, but are often unwilling to keep the reinforcement rate high enough to make a significant impact on their dog's thought process. This often happens because they don't have a detailed understanding of how and when to use food, so they worry more about overfeeding the dog than appreciating the value of using one of the most important resources in a dog's life as a motivator. If you reinforce heavily in the early stages of training, you will be able to lessen food rewards that much quicker.

As you progress with your training, you can reduce food rewards, but only after the behavior is strong and well trained in many different situations (i.e., has become generalized). If you use a "trail mix" of different treats when you train, you will hold your dog's attention much better. Your dog is likely to be unimpressed if he gets dry kibble all the time. However, if you mix his kibble in with some of the high-value treats and he gets one of those every now and then, he will gamble that the next reward might be one of the better treats and worth the effort to keep training.

Look at the following list of food rewards and their approximate calorie counts—it should make you feel better that you are not going overboard with the food rewards. Most dogs will quickly burn the extra calories during training, and you can always reduce his total daily food intake to make sure he maintains his figure!

- Low value—¼ Cup Typical Dry Kibble: Equals 90-125 treats and has 90-125 calories.

- Medium value—Natural Balance® Log: One treat cut to pea-size equals one calorie.

- Medium-high value—Turkey Hot Dog: One turkey dog equals 80-100 treats and has 70 calories.

- High value—Cheddar/Jack Cheese: One ounce equals 90-100 treats and has 110 calories.

- High value—Chicken or Turkey White Breast: Five ounces equals 80-100 treats and has 80 calories.

- High value—Vienna Sausages: One sausage equals 30-40 treats and has 40 calories.

Fading Rewards and Variable Reinforcement

Fading rewards simply means reducing the number of times you use a reward (typically a food treat) while training. Variable reinforcement means varying the percentage of times a reward is given following a successful behavior.

The key first step in reducing food rewards after your dog begins to perform the behavior reliably is to begin pairing verbal praise along with your treats. For example, you give a treat and say "good boy" at the same time. Your dog should begin to listen for your praise as you have linked it to a reward. The second step is to periodically use verbal praise without a treat. Now your dog is listening for your praise in anticipation that a treat is coming. The anticipation is what becomes your strong suit. This is what Las Vegas was built on—the anticipation that if you just put one more quarter into the machine, it will pay off!

Once your dog knows a behavior well, and can perform it in many locations and with many distractions, you can fade the use of your marker signal and rewards. In other words, you don't need to click and treat every time your dog sits for you. However, it's also important to pay off every now and then to keep your dog in the game and gambling, "This time might be the time the reward happens, so I'm going to keep doing what I'm doing, just in case."

Here's an example of how you can fade the use of treats when using a verbal marker while teaching a behavior like "Sit":

1. Ask your dog to "Sit."

2. As his butt hits the ground, say, "Good boy," give a treat (praise and treat paired together) and release him with a release cue such as, "All done."

3. Ask your dog to sit again, but just say, "Good boy," without the treat (builds anticipation of the treat), and release him.

4. The next time, give the treat after your verbal praise (score!).

5. Ask for the sit once again and give the treat again after your verbal praise (score again!).

6. Use just the verbal praise for a couple of rounds, and so on until you are only using treats occasionally but still getting good responses from your dog.

7. You can also add in other rewards that your dog likes, such as asking him to sit and when he does, saying, "Good boy," and throwing a ball or playing a little tug. You could also open a door, pet him, or allow him access to something like the car if he enjoys car rides. These are called "real life" rewards, and anything your dog wants or likes can and should become a reward as you progress in your training.

Reducing the use of food rewards should be a goal, but always be ready to go back to using more or better treats when you add more distractions, duration, or distance to a behavior—at least until your dog has a clear understanding that this is the same training as before, just in a different context. If a well-trained behavior falls apart when you go out into the world, that's information for you. It's time to help your dog by going back to food—usually a high value reward.

Once your dog demonstrates that he can stay focused on the task at hand, you can switch to a lower value food as long as you maintain the successes you achieved with the high-value food in that same location or with the same distractions.

Once you have decided to use fewer treats, bear in mind that never using treats again would be like asking yourself to give up ice cream, cake, or other goodies. There is nothing wrong with using food to reward your dog, just use it to your advantage—to help him get better with his skills. Sometimes it is fun to give your dog a treat, just like it is fun for us to get unexpected rewards. Also, if your dog does something really amazing that you would like repeated, then food is the best paycheck you can give him to keep him in your employment.

Your Voice is a Powerful Thing to Waste

As a means of rewarding your dog, your voice is an often-over-looked tool—especially when getting him relax. Most dogs fall into one of two categories: Those who pay attention to and love to hear the voice of a pet parent and those who have learned to ignore it over time. Obviously you want to be in the first category so you need to learn to use your voice at the right time to help in reaching your training goals.

A dog in the first category has learned to love the sound of his owner's voice because it is connected with things that dogs enjoy most, such as, "Want a cookie?" or "Go for a walk?" In other words, the voice is associated with things the dog enjoys. A dog who has learned to ignore his owner has probably heard the same old thing, over and over again, "Rex, Rex, Rex, heel, right here. Heel, heel, heel Rex!" All the while Rex is busy pulling to the nearest dog park to hook up with his buddies and wondering what the heck you are babbling about back there at the other end of the leash. Unfortunately, this can lead to the owner escalating the tone and loudness of his voice to this "unresponsive dog," a situation which does not lead to a calm dog or a relaxed human.

Whichever category your dog falls into, rest assured your voice has meaning him, so be sure to use it wisely. If he is doing something you want him to do, use your voice to reinforce him. On the flipside, if you don't want your dog to do something, be silent. If a behavior is not reinforced, your dog is likely to skip that one for behaviors that do work to get attention or what he wants.

Danielle uses her voice to acknowledge when Sadie relaxes and makes eye contact, a behavior that Danielle wants to reinforce.

Body Language as a Training Tool

Believe it or not, your body can be a great communication tool for training your dog. The way you stand, the way you move, as well as your stride, can tell your dog to come in closer, move away, or turn and leave the scene.

As you have learned, dogs communicate with one another using their bodies, vocalizations, and some marking behaviors, so it is easy to imagine that our companion dogs are also trying to communicate with us in the only way they know how. Unfortunately, for all their effort to explain themselves, the "Canine to Human Language Conversion Dictionary" is not available and a lot of information is lost in the translation from species to species.

An important piece of training is how you hold your body— how you stand, how you present food rewards when your dog is in the correct position, and how you move around your dog.

For example, dogs pay attention to our shoulders (just as they watch the shoulders of fellow canines) as a clue to which direction we would like them to go. If you and your dog face in the same direction with your dog's shoulders aligned with your leg at one side or the other, this tells him you are going to move forward. Clear enough, but if you lean over him while presenting a food reward or step toward him as he sits in front of you, he thinks you want him to move away.

An often-observed example of this is during leash walking. When your dog is in the correct loose-leash stance at your side, and your food reward is in your hand on the other side of the dog, if you turn and lean over to reward him, your shoulders push toward him. Your dog's reaction will likely be to move away from you. It's no wonder so many dogs choose to be out in front all the time—they are confused by all of our mixed messages.

Betty begins to move away as her owner leans over her.

If you think that is confusing, just think what it must be like for the dog when we face them while calling them to us! We are telling them with our body language to move aside or go away by approaching them head on, but calling them with our voices to come to us! Way weird.

As you begin training the upcoming exercises, you will get a sense of how your body will play a part in helping your dog understand what you would like from him.

Less Commanding, More Rewarding

Dogs who are persistently manipulated with verbal commands, equipment, and physical prompting to perform behaviors (such as pushing them into a sit) become reliant on their pet parents to do everything for them. This is equal to doing a child's homework for him or her. A child might get better grades if an adult did his homework, but he or she would not learn the skills needed to function successfully in the world. This same concept is also true for your dog. If you have been doing his "homework" via constant reminding or demanding obedience, telling him, "No," all the time, and/or using leash manipulations and physical prompts to keep him in line, he will not have learned the skills needed to function calmly in life.

Dogs, like children, must learn to problem-solve when life comes at them, and providing your dog a motivation to perform behaviors through rewards will help him learn those skills. In order for that to happen, however, he will need different, and well-practiced behaviors that will give him the answer to the question, "What do I do when (fill in the blank) _____?" If your dog's current answer to that question is to spiral up and become wild, out of control, inattentive, or reactive, he has very few tools from which to choose.

When your dog has a limited number of tools, he will continue to use the ones that are the most readily available and familiar since those are the easiest to grab. If your dog's behavior toolbox includes impulsive or reactive behaviors and little else, he has no choice but to use the tools that have served him best in the past.

For training to be effective, your dog needs to learn how to handle different situations without grabbing the old tools from his toolbox. Those old tools will always be there, but as you teach your dog that he will be rewarded for calm and relaxed behaviors, those old tools will be buried deep at the bottom of the toolbox under all the new ones, making access to them difficult and unlikely.

A Note on How Long to Train

As you train with your dog, it is important that you don't overdo the amount of training. Science has shown that animals retain better when taught in short (five to fifteen minutes) spurts, rather than long, drawn out sessions. Dogs not only fill up on treats, they also get bored during long training sessions. If you overtrain, your dog will not be as excited about doing an exercise the next time. If you stop before he gets full or bored, leaving him wanting more, you will have a cooperative dog the next time you train with him.

If you find yourself overtraining because you are excited about your dog's progress, simply count out 20-50 tiny treats and stop when they are gone. That will keep you on track with limiting the amount of time you train.

INTRODUCTION TO PART 2

Part 2 of this book will provide you with numerous hands-on training exercises you can use to help calm an overly active or stressed-out dog. In my experience, most of the problems people have with out of control dogs can be solved by mastering these exercises. The exercises are designed to teach your dog how to calm down, pay attention to you, and respond with a new set of skills to every day situations with confidence and composure. These include:

- Choosing to relax instead of engaging in "wild" behaviors.

- Focusing on you instead of other distractions through name recognition and the ability to maintain eye contact.

- Learning how to sit and keep sitting.

- Targeting.

- Greeting strangers calmly.

- Learning to remain calm when the doorbell rings, when getting on the leash, and when out for a walk.

- Accepting handling and restraint from you and strangers.

The exercises are organized like this:

- A brief description of the exercise and how it relates to calming your dog.

- A list of the significant benefits to be gained by teaching the exercise.

- An overview of what you will need in terms of treats, equipment, helpers, and training locations.

- A discussion of the prerequisite behaviors, if any, your dog needs to know before teaching the exercise.

- The approximate amount of time it will take to teach the dog the behavior.

- A detailed step-by-step plan to accomplish the exercise.

- Along the way there are helpful reminders I call "Keep in Mind" designed to provide additional information and helpful hints as you work with your dog.

- At the end of each exercise there is a "Problem Solving" section with suggestions on how to resolve many of the most common training challenges.

While most dogs won't need to learn the skills in each exercise in this book, the exercises are designed to build on the previous one. I recommend you completely train each exercise you want your dog to learn before moving on.

Ten Simple Tips for Success with the Exercises:

1. **Set your dog up for success.** As you begin any training exercise with your dog, work in a calm environment that promotes clear thought. Trying to train during a crisis or in an overly stimulating environment is like asking someone to learn to play the piano in a room full of pre-school children during playtime. While ultimately you will want your dog to be able to handle distractions, when you first start training any new skill, try to reduce the chance your dog will be stimulated by something beyond your control.

2. **Don't rush.** Consider how important each behavior is to you. The more important the behavior or the problem you are trying to resolve, the more time you should invest in training each step of the desired behavior. This ensures better results because you create a strong foundation on which the finished behavior rests.

3. **Read the instructions** and the entire exercise before you begin training so you are clear about what each step requires. That way you will have a solid picture of what the behavior should look like when you are finished with each part. If you can't figure out all the parts and components of the completed behavior, it will be difficult for your dog to understand what you are trying to teach him.

4. **Have realistic expectations.** Review your dog's training history. If you are trying to solve a problem, you will need to analyze how long and how strong the unwanted behavior has become. Has your dog gone ballistic when the doorbell rings for years? When dogs repeat behaviors, there must be some sort of reinforcement going on. It's either fun, it results in attention from humans (even negative attention can be rewarding for many dogs), it relieves stress, it makes scary things go away, or it gets results (such as pulling on leash gets the dog where he wants to go), etc. Defining your dog's history will help you plan how many repetitions you are going to need to make progress and counter the undesired behaviors. Recognize a behavior which has been going on for years might take some time before it is replaced in your dog's toolbox. The upcoming exercises will give you guidelines for how much and how long to train, but every dog is an individual, and as such, may need more or less repetitions. You know your dog best, so adjust accordingly.

5. **Be consistent,** and understand your dog's limits while vowing to prevent your dog from practicing any unwanted behaviors with management and prevention. Until you teach your dog the new behavior, use baby gates, crates, leashes, or put your dog in another room if necessary to prevent undesired behaviors such as jumping on guests.

6. **Review the recommended equipment** you will need to start training. Get what you need together for each exercise, and invest in a treat bag so you can reach your treats quickly during training.

7. **Prevent your dog** from becoming overly aroused or stressed when you are training. To accomplish this, you will need to learn to watch your dog for calming behaviors and signs of stress, such as those mentioned earlier in the book.

8. **Don't jump ahead in your training.** If your dog can't do the behavior in the comfort of his home or yard with ease, don't try to take it on the road. If that means forgoing walks because he reacts toward other dogs, pulls, or bites the leash, you will need to fill that gap with other things that will help him stay focused both mentally and physically until he is able to stay calm and relaxed as you increase the stimulation, a little at a time. Completing the upcoming exercises will help your dog accomplish all of that.

9. **Don't train if you feel stressed.** This is important since dogs often sense human emotions. Are you still feeling pressure and stress when you take your dog out and work with him in public? If so, it's okay to go home, or just work at home until your dog is ready. Remember to breathe and don't rush things.

10. **Find things that motivate your dog.** You need a way to communicate with your dog that he did the right thing. Rewards are in the eye of the beholder (rewards don't always need to be food, but as stated before, it's a good place to start with most dogs), so find things your dog loves and then lavish them on him in the early stages of training so he feels a significant emotional connection between the behavior and the reward. Once you have your dog doing well at one level, raise the bar a little and train the next piece well before moving forward. Be sure as you add each new part, that you go back and throw in a few easy things now and then so your dog is drenched in success—he does not always have to work on something more difficult. Most important, have fun with your dog!

Exercise 1

Relax on a Mat

I begin with this training exercise for all of my human clients wrestling with dogs who can't relax and engage in what, for the humans at least, are troublesome behaviors. The primary goal of this exercise is to teach your dog to choose an acceptable behavior—in this case, relaxing on a mat—when he is not sure what to do. As this will be the first behavior you train, my experience is that it is likely to become one of your dog's strongest default behaviors (instead of jumping on you or barking, for example). Replacing your dog's wild behavior with a default behavior that is calm and relaxing will solve many of your problems.

If you teach your dog nothing else during his life, teach him this exercise and you will reduce your dog's stress and attention-seeking behaviors by noticeable amounts. Your dog will learn a skill that will help him relax his body, rather than getting excited or demanding when you are not paying attention to him.

One of the unique aspects about teaching this behavior is that I *do not* recommend you put it on cue. In other words, you won't be telling the dog to "Relax on a Mat," or "Go to Your Bed," or giving the dog a visual signal. Instead, the dog will *perform the desired behavior on his own*. The reason you want your dog to make the choice to relax on a mat rather than you asking for the behavior, is that many dogs become perplexed when their humans ask them to do certain behaviors at what they perceive to be the "wrong time," such as when the doorbell rings.

While the dog may be willing to go lie down, he still may feel anxious, worried, or excited—therefore from the dog's perspective *it is* the wrong time. This can take a toll on your relationship with your dog and cause him to give pause in future situations when you ask for some behavior and he remembers back when your decisions might not have been in his best interest (at least in his mind).

Harley has chosen to relax on a mat while her owner reads.

Goals

- Make the mat a rewarding and relaxing place for your dog.

- Learn a behavior that by definition promotes calmness.

- Generalize the behavior.

Benefits

- Relaxing on the mat can become an alternative to activities such as whining, jumping, barking, pawing, pacing, stealing items, dropping the ball in your lap repeatedly, and other annoying, reactive, or anxious behaviors.

- This exercise will empower your dog with the ability to calm himself down and enjoy the benefit of relaxing and recuperating his body. It will give your dog something to focus on, as well as give him a way to resolve anxiety or stressors he may encounter in your home or out in the world.

- Relax on a Mat also teaches your dog independence from always being told what to do, and in doing so, builds his confidence when he is able to figure things out on his own. In turn, this supports you and your dog's relationship since you won't have to "command," or tell your dog what to do as "life happens."

- The final benefit of training Relax on a Mat is that it teaches your dog to relax when he is on a leash. The beginning of this exercise is always practiced on leash, teaching your dog to calm down even when he has some restrictions—for example while you are taking him for a walk on-leash.

What you will need

- A portable mat (different from a favorite bed or crate mat), such as a bath towel, bath mat, or a small blanket. If you have tile or hardwood floors, find something that won't slide around.

- Treats: 1/8 cup for toy dogs, 1/4 cup for small dogs, 1/2 cup for medium dogs, and 3/4 cup for large dogs of pea-sized (smaller if you have a tiny dog) medium to high-value treats. These amounts are per training session, although they can be reduced over time. (See Chapter 4 for a list of treats and their values.)

- Something to put your treats in that is easy to dip into and get more as needed (a treat bag is best).

- A six-foot leash and either a harness or a regular collar (no choke chains or pinch collars).

- A quiet, comfortable, indoor place with minimal distractions in which to train. You will train in different locations with more distractions later, which will eventually teach your dog how to relax anywhere, anytime.

Training time

You should do five to ten minute sessions twice a day, at least five days a week. A well-trained behavior should be achieved in just a couple of weeks.

Get the Behavior Started

Step 1—Set up

Put your dog outside, in another room, or in a crate for a few minutes while you get everything ready. Place the mat in front of the chair or couch where you will be sitting, and have it close enough to you that you don't have to stretch over your dog to drop the rewards on the mat.

After you place your mat down, scatter about ten treats on the surface. These are for your dog to find when you bring him back into the room during the first couple of sessions. This will ensure that your dog's initial impression of the mat will be a strong one, and that will have a lasting impact as you continue this training. The first two sessions should be completed within an eight hour period of time. After these first couple of sessions, you will only use treats after your dog has started calming himself or lying down and not plant them on the mat as you did when you first started this exercise.

Step 2—Introduce dog to the mat

It is now time to go and get your dog. Put him on his leash, and then calmly walk back to the area where you placed the mat and allow your dog to find the treats you left.

As your dog discovers the food, sit down in the chair and give him enough of the leash to stand up, sit down, turn, and lie down, but no more. Some people like to hold the leash, others like to step on it, and still others will secure the leash around the leg of the furniture where they are working. By restricting your dog, he will learn to relax while on leash and it will prevent him from wandering away and finding other things in the area that are more interesting than what you are doing together. He will begin to associate being on the mat with good things.

Drop a few pieces of the food on the mat while your dog is busy sniffing around to see if he missed any of the original treats. As your dog is eating those, start to drop one treat at a time, about every one to two seconds around his front paws, also on the mat. Your dog should be getting very interested in what might be making you drop food at his feet! It's important that you drop the treats and not hand them to your dog as that can make many dogs too excited. The idea is to get your dog's head down and more relaxed, not to stare at you.

Step 3—Reward for less intense behaviors

In this early stage of training Relax on a Mat, you are looking for any less intense behaviors than when you first started. Examples of less intense behaviors might be gentle sniffing around the area, sitting, turning his head away, or yawning. Reward each of these behaviors by dropping one piece of food at a time as close to your dog's front feet as possible.

Jessica drops the treats near Harley's feet rather than feeding her directly.

Step 4—Begin to disengage from your dog

Sit back slightly, or turn to the side so you are not looming over your dog, making it clear that you do not intend to interact with him. Once you are seated, pretend you have an invisible dog that you cannot talk to, cannot make eye contact with, or touch. This is very important to the success of this exercise, so be sure to completely disengage from your dog. Again, you want your dog to learn how to calm himself without input or direction from you. The equation for your dog should be, "When my human ignores me, I should calm down and relax because it pays off really well."

Keep in Mind

You might be wondering why you are giving treats when your dog is doing nothing more than sniffing the ground or sitting. The best way to explain this would be for you to consider all the things your dog could be doing besides sniffing the ground, sitting, or lying down—such as jumping up on you, barking at you, whining, chewing his leash, etc. You are rewarding those spaces in time when your dog is actually doing an acceptable behavior (exhibiting relaxed behaviors) in contrast to the ones most people do not want! As you reward these calm moments, the calmness will start to grow stronger because, as you have learned, dogs repeat behaviors that result in rewards.

It may be easier if you have treats in your hand the minute you sit down, as that will allow you to start rewarding immediately, rather than fumbling in the treat container and possibly missing the chance to reward any early calmness. To prevent your dog from discovering the treats in your hand and moving toward you, you can place that hand behind you between rewards. You won't have to do that for long because your dog will discover that you will drop treats only when he is relaxed or calm.

Step 5—Avoid rewarding the dog for staring at you

Now that your dog is figuring out there is something special about being on the mat, try to avoid dropping treats if your dog is staring at you. This is asking a bit more of your dog, as you are now waiting for your dog to relax slightly more, rather than his trying to "make" you give him treats by staring at you. Rewarding when he diverts his attention away from you, helps reinforce that it is the act of simply relaxing, that will be rewarded. (Refer to the Problem Solving Section if this an issue.) With that in mind, drop treats when your dog turns, sniffs the ground, or looks away. This will teach him that looking away or sniffing around for the food is what earns the reward, not staring at you.

Step 6—Slow rewards and wait for sits or downs

Once you get to the point where your dog seems to understand that less activity is what is causing you to be a treat dispenser for him (usually after at least fifteen treats), you can now begin to reward only when your dog is sitting. Some dogs will lay down at this point. Since this is the end goal of this exercise, skip to Step 7 if this happens. In either event, you want your dog to learn how to calm himself, not have you tell him.

Now slow the pace of your rewards. At this point, most dogs will sit while waiting for a treat. Make sure you reward your dog once he begins to sit. When he is sitting voluntarily on a consistent basis, slow the pace of rewards once again and watch what happens. Many dogs will then choose to lie down. If he does, reward him immediately for that behavior. Once he chooses to lie down, stop rewarding him for just standing or sitting on the mat.

Step 7—Randomize rewards and end session

Once your dog has started lying down on the mat during your training sessions, and seems to be more relaxed, you can be more random with the timing of the food rewards. One time you can do a couple of fast ones, then put a few seconds between the next one, then go back to the rapid fire treats, and so forth. It's important to keep your dog guessing as to when the next treat will happen, so he learns to relax even more, in hopes that you will drop the next reward. Just don't hold out *too* long in these early stages. You don't want your dog to worry or become anxious about why you haven't rewarded him in a while as long as he is engaging in a calm behavior.

After five to ten minutes of training say, "All done." Finalize your "All done" by turning your head, yawning, or taking a deep breath to communicate that you *really* are done. Be sure to resist engaging with your dog until you have put everything away, and even then, you should remain quiet and composed so as not to get him worked up all over again. It's important your dog understands that training will stop when you say, "All done," so he is a little disappointed you are no longer going to engage with him. This helps ensure that the next time you bring out the mat he will be more willing to focus and find out what makes you drop the treats. Remove the leash and put everything up until the next time, remembering that session two should be completed within an eight hour period to have the maximum impact on your dog.

Keep in Mind

You are well on your way to teaching your dog how to calm himself down. However, if at any time your dog gets up from the down position after this level of progress, take a deep breath, turn your head away and stop dropping food. Let your dog process this and figure out it was the lying down that was making you drop the treats. It only takes a couple of times for most dogs to have the light bulb go on and decide this is very easy to do and it pays off big!

Building the Behavior

Step 8—Relax onto one hip

As you progress, think about advancing the behavior a little each time you come back and train. The next goal might be for your dog to shift his weight onto one hip, which is a much more relaxed state for dogs (some dogs will lie with their legs splayed like a frog as they relax and that is okay as well). After you reward the initial down, then slow the rewards again to the more random two to five second range until you start to see your dog shift his weight, even just a little, then speed up the rewards again so your dog can arrive at the conclusion that shifting his weight makes you drop the rewards faster again.

As with each piece of this exercise, don't go back and reward previously achieved behaviors. Only reward your dog when he is on his hip if that is what he has offered. Stay at this level for a couple of days until you have reduced the reinforcement rate to the random reward schedule. Your dog should stay for two to five second intervals between rewards.

Step 9—Reward for relaxed signs

Once you have your dog on his hip, you can then wait for an even more relaxed state by rewarding your dog for looking away from you or lowering his head and resting it on the mat. To achieve this, you will slow down your rewards again until you see your dog's head turn or dip toward the mat, and then speed up the reinforcements again once he has offered one of those postures. By taking deep breaths or yawning several times you will help your dog relax faster, so be sure to add that to your training. When your dog can lay down on a hip and not stare, you are ready to add new locations and distractions.

Raising the Bar

You can start to raise the bar by adding more time between treats, distractions, or a new location. Only add one of these components at a time or it might be confusing and your dog may not want to continue with his training if he thinks it's not fun or he has to work too hard.

Step 10—Practice in new locations

Each time you move to a new location, go faster with your rewards for the first ten to fifteen seconds after your dog has laid down, and then slow it down again. Be sure to practice for a couple of days in each new location before moving to the next one.

The more you practice this exercise, the more your dog will understand the finished behavior: "When my human sits down and ignores me, I lay down, and great things happen." Be sure to practice this training in many different areas of your home before you take it on the road. Do not try locations outside your home, however, until your dog has started lying down on his hip and not looking at you.

Step 11—Add distractions

Once you think your dog can do the complete exercise just about anywhere in the house, try doing it in the backyard, or the patio, or even in the car if your dog is wild in the car (not driving, just parked for now). As the locations become more difficult, especially those that come with environmental distractions such as people or other dogs, be sure to speed up your rewards in the early stages. Act as if your dog just started the part where he is lying down so he gets a high rate of reinforcement in the beginning and then wait for the hip movement and finally looking away. Once you have the completed behavior, move to the variable rate of reinforcement after you see that he understands you are doing the same exercise, just in a different place. This usually will happen swiftly if you have trained it well in the original quiet locations.

Step 12—Practice without a mat

After your dog has learned to relax on the mat with ease, do it without the mat occasionally so he learns that when he relaxes, rewards happen even without the visual cue of the mat. Back this up by rewarding your dog any time he chooses to relax and you will create a dog who knows how to calm himself down and has a default behavior of lying down when he is not sure what to do. Only do this, however, after your dog thoroughly knows the exercise with the mat. If your dog offers this behavior randomly without the mat, do acknowledge it with quiet praise, or an occasional treat, but don't reward the same way you do in training or your dog will become anxious about offering the behavior all the time and that is not the objective.

Step 13—Switching to off-leash

To further this training, switch to not using a leash and practice around the house by rewarding your dog for lying on the mat when you bring it out. Switching to off-leash is a great way to teach clingy dogs how to distance themselves from their humans—just put the mat a little farther away each time and get really good at tossing treats to your dog at a distance. It won't take long for your clingy dog to "want" to be away from you.

Step 14—Practice while standing in place

Finally, practice this exercise on-leash again, but now do it while you stand in place, and without the mat. This will teach your dog how to be calm on a leash when you are standing—a great skill for any dog when out in public.

Practice standing with your dog on leash by starting at the beginning, as if your dog has never done this before, then progress ahead at your dog's pace. If he gets it quickly, move along fast, but if it takes your dog some time to understand that you are doing a similar training exercise, that's okay, just go at his pace. Continue until you are getting the default down again, but now you are standing with your dog on his leash. This will help your dog learn to relax and lie down when you are out in public and have him on a leash. Be sure to practice or generalize this behavior all over the house before taking it on the road, just as you did with the other parts of this exercise.

Problem Solving

Dog gets up from the sit or a lie down.

If your dog gets up at any time, take a deep breath and stop feeding until he sits again. If sitting is the standard or criteria you are working on with your dog, you will only reward sitting.

Once you have progressed to where lying down is your new criteria, you may find that your dog will continue to offer a sit because he has been rewarded for that previously. Wait it out. It won't take long before your dog gets bored and lies down. If that happens, reward quickly again by dropping treats between his front paws about one per second for at least ten to fifteen treats and then you can start to slow it down again. Remember, at this stage you will only reward when your dog lies down, since you have now established that as the standard.

Dog rushes your hand every time you drop the treat.

If you find after your dog has eaten the treat you dropped on the mat he gets up each time or is rushing to your hand to get the next treat, try placing the food directly on the mat. While sitting, bend down and place the treat, rather than drop it, so your dog has to follow your hand all the way down to the floor. This will make it easier for him to remain in the sit or down position. If you use this method to deliver your rewards, try to sit all the way back up in your chair between rewards so your dog sees you in an upright position, which is how you will be sitting under normal circumstances. Then remain sitting until the dog gets back into a sit or down position before rewarding again. If you work on this while bending over the whole time, your posture will be part of the visual cue your dog expects to see before he does the exercise in the future. That might cause him to get up in anticipation of getting a treat.

Sitting back in your chair between rewards is important, as you don't want to be leaning over your dog.

Dog does not lie down after ten minutes.

If during Step 6 your dog has not been able to lie down after ten minutes of trying, it is time to stop and take a break. It doesn't matter where your dog is at this point in the training, you want him to be a little disappointed that you are going to end the exercise, not have him filled up on food and/or bored by the exercise. Try training again later and be patient. Your dog will eventually lie down if you work through the exercise as explained. If you come back and work on this within an hour or two, your dog will be a little full and shouldn't be as excited about the food and may become bored enough to lay down. You can also train at times when your dog is sleepier.

Dog seems frantic about the food.

Be careful that you do not reward any signs of stress or greater activity, especially if your dog seems frantic about the treats. Don't reward him again until he exhibits a calm behavior. Then you may go back to dropping the food on the mat a little faster, and just let him eat, one treat at a time. Once you have placed about ten treats on the mat, say "All done," pick up the mat, and put it away until your next session. This will allow your dog time to calm down and digest some of the rewards so he won't be as frantic about getting the food.

You can also use less valuable food, such as your dog's regular dry food with just a few higher valued treats mixed in, so he isn't quite as interested in the food. Training when your dog is not as hungry, such as after a meal, is also effective.

Dog whines or barks.

If your dog whines or barks, take a deep breath and turn your head to send a clear message that you are not going to interact with him. Try dropping your treats faster when your dog is not whining or barking to help him stay focused on the exercise, rather than demanding the food. You can always end the session if your dog seems to be overly anxious. Wait an hour or so and try again.

Dog jumps up on you.

If your dog jumps on you during this exercise, gently stand up, turn slightly away (be sure that you don't make eye contact or talk to your dog) and allow your dog to slide off you then sit right back down. Be sure not to push with your hands, as that can be exciting or arousing for many dogs and the intent is to work toward calmness, not escalate his excitement. It might be necessary to stand up a couple of times before your dog gets the message that you are not going to interact with him, although most dogs get the message pretty quickly. Drop several treats in a row just as you are sitting down again, to keep your dog in the "four on the floor" position.

Dog chews on leash.

If your dog chews on the leash, use a taste deterrent such as Bitter Apple™, or buy a chain link leash to use for this exercise so biting on the leash is no longer fun. Remember that leash biting is usually a sign of stress, so helping your dog understand what you want through quick reward delivery should help him get into the game and leave the leash alone.

Other uses for Relax on a Mat

- If your dog begs at the table, teach him that relaxing on his mat is much easier than putting all the effort into begging. Begin by placing the mat near the chair where you usually sit at the table. In the beginning, do this when you are not eating a meal so it's easier for your dog. After a couple of rounds without a meal on the table, add a meal with only you (add family members later) and reward him for lying on the mat while you eat. When your dog is able to remain on the mat while you eat, graduate to having a family meal, if that's the goal. You will still be working with your dog's leash at this point, but as you will see, the leash will not be needed once you have trained this well.

• If you would like your dog to stay out of a certain area, such as the kitchen, when you are working, place his mat at the edge of the kitchen or just inside an adjacent room and reward any time he is on his mat, but ignore him if he gets off. Your dog will quickly learn that being on the mat, even when you are working in the kitchen, will pay off, and he will figure out that chilling out on the mat is much easier than bothering you.

Exercise 2

Name Recognition

Why is it so valuable for your dog to stop what he is doing and give you immediate attention whenever and wherever you say his name? Because when your dog is focused on you and has learned that this is a rewarding thing to do, he won't be engaging in other behaviors that you might find less desirable. This behavior will help your efforts to develop a calmer dog. Teaching Name Recognition will give you a new way to communicate with your dog. When he hears his name, he should turn and look at you. It gives you a way to "tap your dog on the shoulder" so to speak, and remind him that focusing on you will be rewarding.

This exercise teaches your dog to quickly respond to his name the first time you say it, even if he is distracted or not at all focused on you. It is critical that you learn to be consistent in how you use his name so that it does not lose its power. Remember dogs don't generalize things that are not important to them, so using his name in many different situations and for a variety of reasons may cause his name to become nothing more than white noise. Trying to get his attention by using something other than his name can also cause problems. Think about the word, "No!" That one word is used so frequently and in so many situations to get a dog's attention that some dogs think their name is "No," and many a cartoon has been designed around that very idea. The same thing can happen with his name, so you will want to use it when you really do want his attention and the resulting calm behavior it creates.

Goals

- Your dog quickly responds by turning toward you when he hears his name.

- Once the dog has learned to turn toward you he remains calmly focused on you.

- The dog can perform this behavior in new locations and with distractions.

Benefits

- This gets your dog's focus back on you when he is distracted, straining on the leash toward something, or during those "frozen in time" moments when your dog appears to be about to make an unwise decision, such as barking at something.

- Once the behavior is mastered, no training tools or devices are necessary—your voice alone will be all you need.

What you will need

- A clicker. A verbal marker is not recommended in this exercise.

- Treats: 20-30 medium to high-value treats. (See Chapter 4 for a list of treats and their values.)

- Something to put your treats in that is easy to dip into and get more as needed (a treat bag is best).

- A six-foot leash and a harness, or a limited-slip collar, or a regular buckle collar.

- A quiet, comfortable, indoor place with minimal distractions in which to train. You will train in different locations with more distractions as you progress, which will eventually teach your dog how to respond to you anywhere, anytime.

Training time

You should do five to ten minute sessions two to three times a day, at least five days a week. You can also work this into your day, whenever your dog is not paying attention. Be sure to have rewards with you whenever you are going to say your dog's name and expect a response. A well-trained behavior should be achieved in just a couple of weeks.

Get the Behavior Started

Step 1—Say your dog's name and reward for looks and turns in your direction

You will begin close to your dog. Two to three feet is a good distance. Wait until your dog is looking away and then, clearly and with a friendly voice, say your dog's name—*one time only.* Just as your dog begins to lift his head or turn in your direction (don't hold out for the full turn just yet) you will click and hand your dog a treat right next to your body so he learns to move in close to you for his reward. Smile and tell your dog what a good boy he is, then wait for him to get distracted before saying his name again. When you are done, use a release cue such as "All done."

Step 2—Reward for movement toward you

As you make progress, you should begin to see your dog turning faster and faster after he hears his name. Once you have concluded your dog understands he should turn when he hears his name, begin to click and reward him only as he starts to move toward you.

The goal is to have your dog turn quickly toward you when you say his name.

Step 3—Practice with a leash on

Continue on as you did with Step 2, but now practice with his leash on. This is so his equipment doesn't distract him when you begin working with real environmental distractions outside of your home. If your dog is overly excited by the leash, clip it on and just let him drag it during the exercise until he calms down enough to realize you are not going for a walk.

Building the Behavior

Step 4—Mark and move away to deliver reward

Have several treats in your hand, but don't show them to him. When your dog is not looking at you, say his name and click as he starts to turn in your direction, but this time, take 1-3 steps away from him so he has to turn his head *and* move toward you for the reward. Be sure you have left enough room behind you so you can step away from your dog, and be careful as you back up so you don't run into or over something.

Step 5—Rewarding calm approaches only

Once your dog is moving toward you after hearing his name, click and reward him only when he approaches you calmly. You do not want to reinforce him for lunging at or jumping up on you. Many dogs will approach and sit at this point, so you might want to hold out for that behavior or you may be satisfied with rewarding a calm stand. It's up to you.

Keep in Mind

As you progress in your training, vary the number of steps you move away as well as the speed of your steps so your dog learns to keep pace with you in a number of different situations. This will help him to be prepared for when you take this on the road.

Raising the Bar

Step 6—Adding distractions

Once you see that your dog is really starting to move toward you without hesitation as you step away, you can set up some training sessions with distractions, such as practicing with other people or dogs nearby. Start with low-level distractions, or enough distance so your dog can respond when you say his name. In other words, if your dog goes crazy when seeing another dog that is close to him, you would want to start far enough away so he can still respond when you say his name. The same will be true with people if your dog loves to greet them. When adding distractions, warm up by doing several repetitions at the easier levels (work closer to your dog) before increasing the difficulty in your training session.

Step 7—Adding new locations

Now work on the behavior in new locations. Stick close to your home for the first few sessions to gauge if your dog is able to respond with the higher level of distractions the outside world offers. On an ongoing basis, work on name recognition any time you are out with your dog in a new place.

Problem Solving

My dog doesn't respond to his name, no matter how many times I say it.

During your training, it's important to resist saying your dog's name more than one time. If your dog doesn't respond the first time you say his name, you need to assess why. Does he need more practice in a less distracting environment? Are you too far away? Have you been training too long? Is he full? Is the environment more interesting than you or your treats? Look for reasons and be willing to adjust. If your dog doesn't respond to his name the first time, give him two to three seconds to respond, since he might just be thinking. However, if he doesn't respond after that amount of time, simply tell him, "All done," and take a little break. Your dog should be disappointed that you have ended the training session and when you come back to train again, he'll be more attentive.

My dog does fine with name recognition in the house, but is deaf when I take him outside.

If your dog is highly distracted while on walks and you are unable to get his attention the first time you say his name, this tells you that he is not ready for this level of distraction. You will need to build on his successes in an easier environment or use higher value treats when you take your training out of his comfort zone. Go slow with this and lay that solid foundation before trying to build a skyscraper on top of it. Try training in the back yard or front porch with his leash so he can get the feel of working outside with his equipment, rather than trying to go for a walk and do this training. If you get success in the back yard, try the front porch, and if you get success on the front porch, take a few steps away and train there. Remember, every dog is different and you may have to train each part of the exercise more, in less distracting environments before you can use this on your walks.

My dog only responds when I show him that I have food.

It's essential to resist showing your dog the food in your hand as an attempt to lure him to you. The idea is for your dog to work to get the marker and then be rewarded with food. If you hold the treats out before your mark, your dog will quickly learn that it's only worth his time if he can see the food in your hand and that would be counterproductive to your training. The goal is to strive to use less food once the behavior is effortless, not have to have it all the time to achieve results.

EXERCISE 3

AUTOMATIC EYE CONTACT

Don't you just love to watch dogs that are walking next to their pet parent, lovingly looking up at them every few steps? Or those dogs who sit at street corners and then check in with their handler, waiting for permission to cross? This exercise teaches your dog to "check in" with you anytime he wants something, (such as going out a door) or is not sure how to respond to a distraction in the environment (like another dog walking down the street). Like Relax on a Mat, this behavior is taught without a verbal cue. Your goal here is to make seeking eye contact with you so rewarding that your dog will choose to do it often and in a variety of environments.

Teaching your dog to "check in" through Automatic Eye Contact with you can be a brilliant way to teach calm responses and keep your dog's attention even when there are exciting things happening around him. It is also a wonderful way for your dog to learn that he can make things happen by just looking at you. Ideally, your dog will learn this so well, he won't have to think about it when he wants something—just make eye contact with you and the world is his. It's like providing your dog with a way to ask your permission for the things he would like in life rather than making poor decisions or forging forward on his own.

Sadie pays close attention to Danielle as they practice Automatic Eye Contact.

Goals

- Your dog learns to check in with you, no matter what is going on around him.

- Your dog learns that giving you eye contact is a rewarding behavior.

Benefits

- This powerful tool should be high on your priority list of things to teach your dog, and one to use as a precursor for all the things your dog would like in life. In other words, your dog will believe he can make you put his food down, make you open the door, make you play ball, or make you step forward during your walks together, if he "checks in" with you by establishing eye contact.

- The best thing about teaching Automatic Eye Contact is you can use real life desires as your dog's reward. Once your dog has had a couple of weeks learning this, begin to use Automatic Eye Contact for all the things your dog wants. If your dog wants to go outside, wait for eye contact before you open the door. Get eye contact when you are going to feed your dog each day. Looking at you will make you put the bowl down. If your dog wants to sniff around or urinate while out on walks, get eye contact and then give permission to do those things. In other words, teach your dog that checking in with you makes all the things he loves happen!

• This is a multifaceted behavior that can be used in many different distracting situations such as leaving food that is dropped on the floor or not chasing a ball.

• This exercise also teaches your dog to become more comfortable with people looking directly at him or while approaching him.

What you will need

• A clicker or a verbal marker if you prefer.

• Treats: 20-30 medium to high-value treats.

• Something to put your treats in that is easy to dip into and get more as needed (a treat bag is best).

• A six-foot leash and a harness or regular collar. For this exercise, it is best if you practice this both on and off-leash, so your dog has practice with and without his equipment. That way, when you begin to work outside of your home, he will already feel comfortable doing this with his leash on, giving you one less step to work through later.

• A helper for Steps 9 and 10.

• A quiet, comfortable, indoor place with minimal distractions in which to train. You will train in different locations with more distractions as your progress, which will eventually teach your dog that the answer for everything is to look at you.

Training time

Count out five to fifteen treats and train until those are gone, practicing two to five times each day, while making sure to move around to different locations as you practice. This will help your dog to generalize the behavior to many different areas. If you can do this five times a week, a well-trained behavior should be achieved in just a couple of weeks.

Get the Behavior Started

Step 1—Show your dog you have treats

Take several of what you typically use for treats in one hand and a clicker in the other unless you are using a verbal marker. Then show your dog some of these wonderful goodies by passing your open hand with the treats past his nose so he can see and smell them, then raise your hand high enough that he is unable to get to them. I recommend you hold both arms raised straight out at about chest level (so you look like the letter "T"). Be sure to stand all the way up so you are not leaning over your dog, as you want him to see you in an upright position—how you will be most of the time. Your dog will probably stare at the hand with the food for a few seconds, trying like crazy to figure out how to get it from you. It's important that you stand very still and don't help him in any way.

Danielle shows the correct arm position to use during the early part of this training.

Step 2—Reward initial eye contact

The second your dog looks away from the food and toward your face, mark and reward him by taking a piece of food from your hand, feed him, and do it all over again. It doesn't matter, at this early stage, if your dog doesn't look directly at you. It's good enough if he looks in the general direction toward your face. The idea is to get him to stop looking for or staring at the food and to look toward you for some guidance. As soon as that happens, he will get the marker and the reward he was fretting over.

Be patient and watch carefully so you can capture that exact moment your dog looks toward your face. Look for his eyes to shift toward you—it does not need to be his head turning, but try not to miss any of those first glances or shifts as he may become confused as to what you want. Practice this in one location for about five to ten rewards, then release him with "All done," and take a short break. If, after a few times of doing this, your dog doesn't bother to look at the food, rather he looks right at you when you stretch your arms out, then mark, and reward! That is exactly what you want!

Keep in Mind

Work when you are calm and relaxed, and be sure to take a few deep breaths as you begin to train. Also, remember to smile since you want your dog to see a happy face, not a grumpy one, when he turns to make eye contact with you.

Step 3—Switch hands

For your next training session, you should switch hands with the food. Many dogs are right or left-pawed, so you might see the behavior speed up or slow down. The idea is your dog understands checking in with you is a good thing, no matter which hand the food is in or where you are standing. Practice at this level for about five to ten rewards, and then take a short break. Your dog should have a good understanding at this point that the marker happens when he looks away from the food and toward you.

Step 4—Get your dog's full and direct eye contact

You will now work to get your dog to make more direct eye contact, not to just look away from the food. To get direct eye contact, you again pass the food by your dog's nose, but this time you will have food in both hands. Your dog will probably then look back and forth trying to guess the correct answer. If your outstretched hands are at chest level, he will have no choice but to look toward your face as he is shifting back and forth between your two hands. You will use your marker as he looks at your face. Mark even a tiny eye shift toward your face. Don't hold out for the entire behavior if he doesn't get it at first, you will get there soon enough. By marking for eye contact, your dog will have an understanding that looking or glancing at you will make you mark, and then he gets the reward. Of course, if your dog makes full-on eye contact right away, mark and reward that. It shouldn't take too many repetitions to get your dog's full eye contact, but always be sure to go back to easier steps if he is having any difficulty.

Building the Behavior

Step 5—Add eye contact duration

You should be receiving consistent, (even if it is brief) eye contact from your dog before you try to add duration. If he can look away from the food eight out of ten times in a row (or never look at the food in the first place), and give you direct eye contact, you are ready to add this step. Begin the new training session with food in one hand again, and then after your dog makes eye contact, delay your marker for at least one second, as long as he keeps looking at you. Strive for one to two seconds of eye contact for five to ten repetitions. Once your dog is good at this, you can add a little more time as you train.

Keep in Mind

Be sure to mix it up. Sometimes mark fast, while other times hold out for slightly longer periods. If at any point your dog seems confused, make the time shorter for a couple of tries, and then gradually add a little more time.

Step 6—Fade out your outstretched arms

Now that your dog can look at you for longer durations, it is time to be less exaggerated with the food in your hands. This is to help your dog learn to make eye contact with you all the time, not just when you are standing with your arms out to your sides. Start with less exaggeration by holding the hand with the food in front of your stomach area, rather than out from your side. After you show your dog the treats in your hand, close your fist around the treats and bring your hand up to your stomach area. Mark and reward when your dog looks away from your hand and looks up to make eye contact. He will have to shift his eyes up, past your hand, which is sometimes hard to see, so work in a well-lit room and pay close attention. Continue at this level for several sessions until your dog is reliably looking at you and not your hands.

Bonnie gets Automatic Eye Contact from Heidi with her arms lowered.

Step 7—Practice with hands behind your back

Putting your hands behind your back or in your pockets will increase the challenge for your dog. The standard and gauge for success is the same—when your dog looks at you, mark and reward the eye contact until he is reliably making eye contact with your hands in your pockets or behind your back. Strive for success at this at least 80% of the time.

Step 8—Practice with no food in hands

Finally, work on not having any food in your hands at all. Rather, keep your rewards in a treat pouch, on a counter, or on a table and wait for the eye contact, then follow through with your marker and reward. Look for success at least 80% of the time.

Raising the Bar

By adding distractions while building Automatic Eye Contact, you will expedite reaching the goal of your dog checking in no matter what is going on around him. It's usually best to teach this part on-leash so your dog doesn't have the opportunity to walk away, especially when you move your training outside.

If at any point you are unable to keep your dog's focus on you, use an easier and less exciting distraction. In other words, if your dog is a nut for a tennis ball, don't start with that as a distraction or you may never get eye contact. Even when you have worked up to the tennis ball, start at a great enough distance so your dog can look away from the distraction and back to you.

It is often easier to have a helper for this part so you can focus on your dog while they introduce the distractions. Your helper can be one of the distractions if your dog loves to greet people. Start with easy distractions that he won't be overly enthusiastic about, such as an old toy that has lost its appeal, or have your helper stand at a far enough distance that your dog remains calm if he is a people-loving dog. Using distractions that are easy in the beginning and grow more difficult will make it easier for your dog to keep his attention on you each step of the way. This will teach him that the rest of the world is a big question mark, but you are the certainty in his life and will mark and reward as he turns his attention back to you.

Training outside means your dog will face a variety of distractions. You need to make Automatic Eye Contact very rewarding when you move outside.

Step 9—Use a toy as a distraction

Put your dog on-leash. When you are ready to proceed, your helper can hold a toy out of reach, but where the dog can see it. If you don't have a helper, just toss the toy far enough away that it is out of your dog's reach. Being on-leash means the dog cannot reach the toy. If he should start to pull toward the object, stand with your arms tucked to your sides and avoid stepping or being pulled forward and allowing him to get to the toy. By holding tight, you will show your dog that his efforts are not going to work. If your dog is powerful, you can tie his leash to a heavy piece of furniture, or loop the handle over the outside of a doorknob and close the door so the leash is secured on the other side of the door. Now, simply wait in silence and use your marker the second he looks back at you to figure out why you are not moving, and then give your dog a treat. Hold the treat close to you so he learns to come back to you each time. Keep working on this step until your dog is easily looking away from the toy and making eye contact with you.

Step 10—Add movement of the toy

Now, have your helper move the toy around a bit (or you pick up the toy and move it around then toss it out of reach) and wait for your dog to check in with you before you mark and reward. Remember to feed your dog right next to you so he learns that his rewards always happen close to you. This will teach him to stay closer in general since he won't want to waste all that energy moving away from you just to have to move back again.

Step 11—Add harder distractions and use high value rewards

After you have successfully kept your dog looking at you with a low-level distraction, you can start to make it harder. The real trick, however, is to have the value of your reward match or exceed the distraction. You can also achieve this by working at a greater distance so your dog essentially calculates that getting to the distraction is not as good an option as sticking with you.

Problem Solving

My dog keeps lunging toward the toy when I try using it as a distraction.

When introducing high-level distractions, it is important that you don't work so close to the distraction that your dog is hitting the end of the leash while trying to get to it. That would be a major punishment for your dog if, every time you work with him, he is being "nailed" by his leash and collar. Instead, introduce things slowly and at a greater distance. The same goes for working with people as your distraction. If people overly excite your dog, just ask your helpers to step further away, and the leash will prevent him from being reinforced by getting to the person.

Exercise 4

Sit and Keep Sitting

This exercise teaches your dog how to remain in place despite distractions and temptations to engage in other behaviors. Generally this is referred to as teaching your dog to "Stay," but I like to think of it as a two step process—getting your dog to sit and then building the duration of the sit. When you teach it this way, what you want the dog to do is clearer to him. Teaching just a "Stay" often involves waiting longer and longer between the moment when the dog sits or lies down and when the reward or praise is given. Often these exercises end with the dog getting up and wandering away or the owner repeating "Stay, stay, stayyyyyyy," over and over while holding out an open palm of the hand as a gesture to remain in place as she tries to step further away. Then if the dog does get up, owners often say, "No, stay," while they run back to their dog to start again. The poor dog ends up being more confused since he is not getting any information to tell him when he has the right answer.

Rather than focusing on "Stay," which most people don't train well, why not teach your dog to Keep sitting (or laying down) until you tell him otherwise?

Goals

- Your dog begins to sit for longer periods of time.

- He can keep sitting even with distractions.

- Most importantly, he can maintain a sit while people approach.

Benefits

- Keep Sitting is a great alternative to otherwise rowdy behaviors such as jumping up on people or scratching at a door.

- Over time your dog will develop a rock-solid sit, which he will use more and more when he is not sure what to do—plus it will generally have a calming influence on him.

- If your dog is nervous or anxious in new settings, Keep Sitting will help your dog to focus on you rather than being concerned about what is happening in the world around him.

What you will need

- A clicker or verbal marker if you prefer.

- Treats: 20-30 medium to high-value treats.

- A six-foot leash and a harness, a limited-slip collar, or a regular buckle collar. You can work with your dog off-leash, but at some point, you will want to train with the equipment he will be wearing out in the world so he becomes familiar with it before you take this exercise on the road.

- A helper or two as you begin to add distractions.

- A quiet, comfortable, indoor place with minimal distractions in which to train. You will train in many different locations with more distractions as you progress, which will eventually teach your dog sitting is a behavior that will be rewarded.

Training time

You should do a couple five to ten minute sessions at least three to five days a week. As you move forward, this exercise should be a part of daily life so your dog learns to offer sits in lots of different situations. Once trained, continue to carry some of your dog's kibble in your pocket and make training Keep Sitting a frequent and random event. This will encourage your dog to always be ready to offer sitting, just in case this is the time you are going to ask him to "Sit." A well-trained behavior should be achieved in just a week or two if you work on this as suggested.

Get the Behavior Started

Teaching your dog to remain in place involves rewarding him for sitting for different lengths of time and until you release him. Once you have that element in place, you will begin adding distractions so he learns to remain steady, even when life is happening around him. Note that we are assuming your dog already has learned at least the basics of sitting when cued.

Step 1—Sit, Reward, "All done"

To begin, cue your dog to "Sit." As soon as he does, mark it, then feed him while adding some quiet praise if you like. Each time you train, it is important that you release your dog from the sit with a cue, such as "All done," and then move to a new location each time, even if it's just a couple of steps away. This will help your dog to generalize the behavior. Ask for the sit again and follow with your marker and treat. Your dog will be thinking, "All I have to do is sit and I get treats? Cool, I can do that all day."

Even a puppy can quickly learn to sit if rewarded with a tasty treat.

Keep in Mind

It's important to mark *before* your food hand begins to move to give the reward. That will prevent your dog from jumping up at your hands and getting out of the sit position. If you have a small dog, bend at the knees to feed so he does not have to jump up to get food. If that is too difficult, you can sit or try kneeling on the ground as you train.

Step 2—Sit in a variety of locations

Work on this behavior in as many training sessions as necessary until your dog can sit for up to five seconds in 20 different places without getting up until you say your release cue. This can take a couple of days or just a few times, depending on your dog and your time. Do not hurry. It's far better to take your time on this part so the sit is a very strong behavior, rather than trying to rush ahead to the next part. The more you train, the more likely you will start to see some immediate results from this exercise—your dog will begin to offer sits all the time to see if this is where the session will start again! That's the kind of results most people want from their dogs!

Step 3—Increasing and varying duration

As you practice, your dog should be catching on that he should keep sitting until you say, "All done." Once you have that component in place, you can start to increase the time between when your dog sits and when you mark and reward. It's important to vary the additional time and not just make it more difficult. One time it can be five seconds before you mark and treat, the next two seconds before you mark and treat, and then back to five seconds before you mark and treat. The important factor here is to keep your dog guessing as to how long he should keep sitting before he hears the marker. This will keep him gambling on the fact that his continued sitting will pay off. Continue to increase the time as you practice with a goal of ten seconds between your "Sit" cue and the marker. Once your dog is steady and can sit for a full ten seconds in 20 locations around your home, you are ready to move to the next step. Remember to mix shorter and longer times so your dog doesn't think it always gets more difficult.

Building the Behavior

Step 4—Add a step back distraction

Now that you are able to vary the amount of time between the "Sit" cue and the mark and treat, you can begin to add small distractions. You are the easiest distraction to add in the early stages, and your dog will enjoy trying to figure out if he should keep sitting, even when you are moving around a bit.

Cue your dog to "Sit" and, just before you are ready to mark and treat, make a slight movement with your foot, as though you were going to step back. If the dog remains seated, you will mark as you move your foot back toward your dog. Then give the treat and release your dog. The idea is that your dog will keep sitting even if you are moving a tiny bit. Be sure to say, "All done" when you are finished or if you believe your dog is going to get up. This will help him understand if he just keeps sitting, even when you step away, that you will come back to him, mark it, and he gets a treat—cool deal, since all he has to do is sit there while you do all the work. Do this small step with one foot about five to ten times, and then try the other foot in the same way.

Step 5—Add more body movement distractions

During the next training session, have your dog sit, and then try taking a small step to one side or raise your arms in the air before you mark and treat. As you add more movement distractions, you may have to move back to your dog faster in the beginning before you mark and treat to keep your dog in place. Move back to your dog each time and don't mark it until you are in feeding range of your dog to prevent him from getting up to get the treat after you said the word or clicked. Release your dog after you feed. This will help your dog learn to wait until he hears the release cue before getting up.

You should be able to progress by adding more of your own body movements, i.e., taking a few steps away, turning in a circle, or other movements, before you mark and treat. I recommend you add these movements piecemeal, for example, doing a quarter turn with your body before turning in a complete circle. Stay at that level until you are convinced he understands that continuing to sit is *still* the answer, then add a half turn, and so on. By taking it slowly and in small increments, you will ensure that your dog is solid at continuing to sit as you add greater distractions.

Step 6—Add other distractions

If you are convinced your dog will keep sitting with the simple distractions you have added, you can include others such as family members walking in the room and food being dropped on the floor just out of his reach. However, keep in mind that you may need to use better rewards and/or a higher rate of reinforcement as you add more difficulty to your training. If your dog keeps getting up, you go back to may need to use easier distractions and build up slowly to the more difficult ones.

If your dog can keep sitting in the presence of another dog or a favorite toy then you can move to Step 7.

Raising the Bar

The following is a difficult skill for most wild and crazy dogs to learn, especially if they have always been able to run and jump up on anyone as they approach. However, by mastering the steps above you have built the foundation for your dog to learn this behavior.

Step 7—Reward on approach

When the above distractions become a "piece of cake" for your dog, make it harder by having friends and family members approach him while you keep him sitting with your marker and rewards. You will practice this part on a leash so your dog is unable to move forward to the person if he should get up at any time. It's important that your dog doesn't "self reward" by getting up and going to the person. As the helper approaches, mark and reward for each step she takes toward your dog. You will be "telling" your dog that the correct behavior is to Keep Sitting, even if someone is approaching you. If your dog looks like he might get up as someone approaches, say "All done" and have the person back away. Try it again with better treats until you can have your helpers move all the way up to your dog and possibly pet him if that is your goal. If petting is too tough, continue to practice just the approach until your dog concludes, "People approach and I get rewards, but if I get up, the treats and the people stop coming."

Even a nine week old puppy can learn to sit when people approach.

Keep in Mind

When beginning to add more significant distractions, avoid the temptation to try to get your dog to sit for long periods of time between the "Sit" cue and the mark/reward. Build the duration up slowly and avoid trying to vary both duration and distractions at the same time at this point. If you are working on distractions, don't also try to add distance from your dog. If you are adding distance, you don't add distractions. Each component must be thoroughly trained before combining.

As you continue, always remember to work at your dog's pace and don't hurry this process. This is a core behavior for teaching your dog he *can* remain sitting no matter what is going on around him and it will take time.

Step 8—Laying down until released

Often you find that a dog who has been released from sitting will remain in that position with the hope that you will continue the training, or you may find that your dog will move from a sit to a down. Take advantage of this and mark and reward if it happens spontaneously. If it continues to happen, add a verbal cue, such as, "Settle," or "Lie down," just as your dog is starting to lie down, then mark and reward it. Go through all of the relevant steps above to train down as its own behavior, adding duration and distractions as noted above. Before long, you will have a nice down with a stay.

Problem Solving

I keep dropping the treats, which makes my dog get up.

Many people find their dogs will get up because they drop treats as they try to deliver them to the dog. If this happens, you can try a couple of things. First, attempt to get your foot over the dropped food to prevent your dog from getting it, so he doesn't get rewarded for getting up. If you say "All done" and prevent him from getting the treat, the next time you drop a treat your dog might conclude it's not worth going after a stray treat since he never gets the ones that drop, but you will make sure he gets them for remaining in the sit. You can also try something easier to hold and less likely to drop from your hand, like a turkey dog that your dog can nibble on, rather than trying to hold a bunch of treats at once.

My dog keeps jumping up toward my hand to get the food and he gets out of the sit.

This can be due to a couple of things. As mentioned before, this is likely due to you not bringing your hand down far enough to your dog's face after marking. Try lowering your hand more or bending at the knees to get closer to your dog's mouth when you feed. But this can also happen when using *too* valuable of food rewards. Some dogs are so excited by the rewards that they are in a hurry to get to them. Try using your dog's regular dry food as the reward for this to see if that helps your dog calm down. Once you are getting success, you can use better rewards when you begin to add distractions.

My dog keeps getting up before I release him.

If your dog gets up before you are ready to release him, tell him "All done" and stop training for a short period of time. When you come back to train, watch for signs that your dog may get up and go faster with your marker and rewards the next time. Also, do much shorter sessions. Your dog might be bored or full.

Exercise 5

TARGETING TO YOUR HAND

This exercise teaches your dog to touch his nose to the palm of your hand on the verbal cue of "Touch." Sounds weird, but this is a wonderful training exercise that gives your dog something to focus on and an alternative behavior to jumping on people, tugging on clothes, or chewing on hands. Giving your dog a way to focus on something other than what is taking place in the environment (which can be very stimulating for some dogs) is the main purpose of this exercise.

Goals

- To present your hand and have your dog actively touch it.

- Have your dog touch your hand on cue while it is moving away.

- To be able to target in a variety of environments and in the presence of distractions.

Benefits

- It is an easy way to teach your dog to come to you. This can help keep him from focusing on other things that might get him excited or overly reactive.

- It can be used to teach other fun skills, such as finding the heel position and going over or under things.

- It is a prerequisite skill needed before moving on to the "Say Hi" behavior taught in Exercise 6, where the dog learns to greet other people.

What you will need

- A clicker or a verbal marker if you prefer.

- Treats: 20-30 medium to high-value treats per session.

- A quiet, comfortable, indoor place with minimal distractions in which to train. Eventually you will train in many different locations with more distance, and teach your dog to touch your hand in the presence of distractions.

Training time

You should do two five to ten minute sessions, at least three to five days a week, as well as integrating this training into your daily life. A well-trained behavior should be achieved in just a few weeks if you work on this as suggested.

Get the Behavior Started

Step 1—Present your hand

Place a few treats in one hand along with your clicker if you are using one. Present your empty hand about three to five inches from your dog's face with your palm facing toward your dog and your fingers straight out but relaxed. Position your body close enough to your dog that you don't have to lean from the waist to reach him because that might make him feel pressure to back away. If you have a small dog, sit, kneel, or bend at the knees so you don't have to bend over your him.

Step 2—Mark/reward a successful touch

Present your empty hand to the dog as described in Step 1. Your dog will likely be curious about what you might have in the hand and will move forward to sniff it. Focus on marking the moment your dog touches your hand, not before or after so it is clear to your dog that he will be rewarded for touching your hand with his nose. It's essential that you simply present your hand and not reach out to your dog once your hand is in front of him. It's your dog's job to move toward and touch your palm, not for you to reach out and touch his nose.

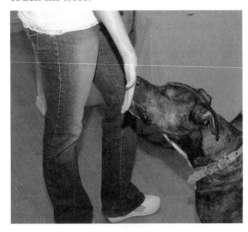

This is the exact moment you want to mark.

Step 3—Multiple touches

After you have marked the touch, bring your empty hand up and away from your dog before you present it again. It's the movement toward your dog's face that will help him learn to touch your hand. Just dangling your hand in front of your dog will not entice his curiosity, but the movement will. Once you have him touching ten to fifteen times in a row, take a short break by releasing your dog with a release cue such as "All done."

Now, instead of holding your hand in front of your dog's face, begin with your hand held up and away from your dog.

Building the Behavior

Step 4—Practice using the other hand

When you come back to train, start where you left off, but switch hands. You want to time your marker as accurately as possible, so pay close attention and mark the second your dog's nose touches your hand. Stay at this level until you can get ten to fifteen nose touches in a row , but do take breaks as needed, so your dog has time to process this new information.

Step 5—Add the cue "Touch" or "Target"

Once your dog is successfully touching your other hand, you can go back to the first hand and then add a cue such as "Touch" or "Target" just before you present your hand. Most dogs really enjoy participating in this exercise, and you can quickly start to move around to different locations. Continue to remain close to your dog as you change locations until you are convinced your dog is responding to your "Touch," cue reliably. Your goal is to get eight out of ten times, in ten to fifteen different locations.

Step 6—Add movement

After you see that your dog understands the verbal cue, start to add a little distance and movement so he has to step toward you in order to touch your hand. Your dog will now have to take a step or two to reach your hand when you give him the verbal cue of "Touch." You can also present your hand near your dog, give the "Touch" cue, but move your hand away so your dog has to follow it to touch. Go slowly, and don't add too much distance at first so your dog can learn to step toward you a little at a time.

See if your dog will move toward you a few steps to target your hand.

Raising the Bar

Step 7—Present your hand at different angles and levels

To make it harder for your dog, add the presentation of your hand at different angles and levels so he sees that touching your hand, no matter where it is at, is the answer. Be sure to keep your sessions short so your dog will be excited to start another round the next time you ask him to touch your hand. Don't be afraid to have your dog jump up to touch your hand as long as he is healthy and doesn't have any problems with his hips or knees. Most dogs love to jump to touch hands, so definitely add this if your dog is capable. It is good exercise and very fun for most dogs.

Step 8—Generalize to new locations

You will do the different variations of "Targeting" all around your home so the behavior becomes generalized. Try for five to ten places each day. You don't have to do many in each location, as you are just showing your dog that you might do this anywhere.

Step 9—Practice on leash

Next, practice with your dog on a leash so he gets the feel of targeting while wearing his equipment. This is important since you will want to be able to use this in public when he is likely to be wearing a leash. If you practice ahead of time, it will be easy for your dog to make the transition.

Step 10—Add distractions

After your dog is successfully touching each time you present your hand, you can add targeting with distractions. Have your dog target your hand in the presence of other people or dogs, but do it at a distance at which your dog can stay focused on you and what you are doing. As you practice, you should be able to move closer and closer to these types of distractions. If you can do this behavior successfully while near a busy dog park then you know you have it made, but it's important, as with all training, that you move through this training at your dog's pace. If he doesn't respond when you get close to a distraction, you are too close. Back away and try again. Make it easier for your dog until he understands that you might ask him to "Touch," even when there are things that interest him. Trained as a step-by-step process, your dog will thoroughly enjoy this new skill and you will have a way of keeping his attention.

Problem Solving

My dog doesn't seem to understand what I want when I present my hand.

If your dog gets stuck and doesn't seem to understand what you want, or if he did target a few times but has now stopped, move around a little to see if a different position will get him get going again. Be sure to work close as you begin training. Making your presentation more animated will often help to get him going again as well. Try presenting your hand first with your fist closed as you bring your hand down, and then open it quickly in front of your dog as if you have something in there that you want him to see. Be sure you are not bending over your dog. Stand tall and bend at the knees or sit if your dog is small. You might also try having your hand behind your back or in a pocket and then presenting it. This will often get your dog to move forward to see if you have something. If these ideas don't work, try presenting your hand to look like you are holding a treat in it, but without the treat. Once you have your dog touching, quickly do another "Touch" to reinforce the behavior.

My dog thinks I'm telling him to shake when I hold out my hand for him to target.

If you have taught your dog to shake he might think that's what you want because it looks similar to holding your hand out for the Target to Hand behavior. Most people teach their dogs to shake with their own dominate hand, so try using the other hand to see if that solves the problem. Once you have it on a verbal cue, you can switch back to the other hand. If you are still having problems after trying the opposite hand, you can solve this by working extra close to your dog (two to three inches away) and presenting your hand so it looks like you have a treat between your fingers, but you won't actually have one. Be sure to stand tall, as most people bend over when asking their dogs to "Shake." That will help your dog understand that you are positioned differently and asking for a different behavior. Continue to do it this way until you have added the verbal cue and then you can begin to open your hand for your dog to target. Say your verbal cue first, then drop your open hand. Your dog should respond to your verbal cue of "Touch" and do the behavior without trying to shake.

EXERCISE 6

SAY HI FOR CALM GREETINGS

Are you embarrassed because your dog approaches people like a Mack Truck? Does your dog jump on people, put his nose where it doesn't belong, or pull you like you are the back end of a sled dog team to greet people? This Say Hi exercise will help your dog pay attention to you, walk calmly up to people and greet them politely by touching his nose to their hands—solving many of the impulse greeting routines that most pet parents find embarrassing or dangerous.

The previous exercises involved interactions between you and your dog almost exclusively. Now we are going to add interactions with other people, making this exercise substantially more challenging in many ways. This exercise will build on the Keep Sitting and the Target to Hand exercises so you will need to have successfully trained those behaviors before moving forward and adding this element. Be sure that both skills have been trained in a variety of places before adding moving on to Say Hi.

Goals

- Your dog keeps sitting while your helper approaches and will touch the helper's hand on cue.

- Your dog can calmly target another person's hand when asked to do so.

- Your dog can Say Hi to new people and in new locations.

Benefits

- The long-term benefit of this exercise is that your dog will no longer feel a need to jump up to greet people. He will learn that he will be rewarded for a more acceptable greeting—a nose touch to the hand. This will allow the dog to satisfy his curiosity about visitors, but he will also learn to come back to you after calmly greeting the new arrival.

- For those dogs who worry about people reaching out to them, this is a great way for them to overcome the fear of hands. These dogs learn to recognize human hands as a target they can touch with their nose and then receive a reward, rather than worrying about being touched by an unknown person.

What you will need

- A clicker, or use a verbal marker if you prefer.

- Treats: 20-30 high-value treats per training session.

- A six-foot leash with your dog on his regular buckle collar, limited-slip collar, or harness.

- Several people who will help you with this exercise. If your dog has a history of reactivity, biting or fear, you should work with a reputable positive reinforcement trainer/behavior expert before using this exercise. (See Resources for website referrals.)

- A quiet, comfortable, indoor place with minimal distractions in which to train.

Prerequisites

Your dog should be able to do both Keep Sitting and Target to Hand behaviors before you work on this exercise.

Training time

Do five to ten minute sessions a couple of times a day at least three to five days a week, as well as integrating training into your daily life. A well-trained behavior should be achieved in a couple of weeks if you work on each section as suggested.

Get the Behavior Started

Step 1—Warm up with Keep Sitting at your side

Warm up your dog with a couple of quick repetitions the Keep Sitting exercise. Practice having your dog sit next to you on the side where he normally walks on-leash. You can choose to add a distraction or duration if you like, but it's not necessary. Keep your warm-up short; spend a minute or two at this level to ensure your dog is "in the game." Most dogs are ready to move forward to the next step quickly, so don't hold yours back by staying at this point too long.

Keep in Mind

"Calm" is the word to keep in mind when teaching this exercise. It's important that you don't move forward until you have a relaxed and calm dog with each of the following steps. This will ensure that you are training your dog to be comfortable with new people, as well as preventing him from jumping on people in excitement.

Step 2—Keep Sitting while people approach

Now practice Keep Sitting with people approaching you as your dog sits at your side. Be sure to select people who will cooperate with your instructions because you do not want someone undoing all your hard work! Start with your dog on-leash and sitting at your side while you reward him for the sit. You may need to have particularly high-value treats for this part if your dog is really excited by people. Have the person approach you, one step at a time. In the early stages, you will mark and treat your dog for every step the person takes toward him, as long as he maintains the sit. Have your helper come close enough to shake your hand. Instruct your helper to refrain from reaching out and touching your dog at this point.

If your dog starts to get up at any time during your helper's approach, have your helper stop, look away from your dog, and take a few steps backward. Then tell your dog "All done." The release makes it clear the person is not coming forward and the treats stop if your dog gets up. Wait at least five seconds and then try again with your helper moving slower, or offering a higher value reward.

Is your dog still sitting? Keep practicing until he is able to remain sitting four out of five times until the person can get to within hand-shaking distance of you.

If your dog gets up as your helper approaches, ask him to stop and then try again.

Step 3—"Touch" the helper's hand

Warm your dog up by practicing a few easy sets of the Target to Hand exercise. Once again, you should have your dog on-leash.

Now ask your helper to stand four to five feet away from you. Have your helper present his or her hand for your dog to target. You will say "Touch" and direct your dog's attention to the person's hand with your own hand. Your dog should be used to following your hand by now, so he should readily step with you. When you can see that your dog is just about to touch your hand, move it out of the way and see if he will touch your helper's hand instead.

Tracy guides Bo to Jason's hand and moves hers just as Bo is about to touch it.

Use your marker to indicate when he touches your helper's hand, but rather than feeding your dog right there, you will instead move back two or three steps, then give him the reward on the side where he normally walks. Your dog should turn from your helper for the reward after he hears the marker. He will now see that he has to move away from the person to get the reward from you. If he is unsure what to do, encourage him to move to you by using a kissy sound or patting your leg (it's okay if you show your dog the reward since he already heard the marker, but make sure you feed him right next to your side). Praise him as he takes his reward, so he understands that he got the correct answer. Step back toward your helper when you are ready to practice again, and have your dog carry out touching your helper's hand for about ten repetitions.

Keep in Mind

Moving away to reward your dog after he targets your helper's hand is a preventive measure. By moving away, it prevents the person from "ambushing" your dog by trying to pet him when he might not be comfortable with that or if it would be too stimulating for him. With this exercise, your dog will be less likely to get aroused or worried if he knows that you will always move him away after the greeting. This is also a very helpful tool for dogs who would normally jump on people, since they don't get the opportunity to linger long enough to jump. They will quickly learn that people are not for jumping on, rather, they are for targeting.

Step 4—Switch the "Touch" cue to a "Say Hi" cue

The reason for switching cues is so your "Touch" cue will still mean to touch your hand, whereas the "Say Hi" cue will mean to touch someone else's hand. It's easier to have each different behavior identified in your dog's mind, so it is clear to him what you want during any level of your training.

To switch the cue, you will use the new cue, "Say Hi" then say the old cue, "Touch," one right after the other as you direct your dog to touch your helper's hand. Practice adding the "Say Hi" cue in front of the "Touch" cue for about ten repetitions with both cues, then switch to using only the "Say Hi" cue the next time. Most dogs complete the behavior without too much thought and you can then use the "Say Hi" cue by itself going forward.

When you present the new cue without the old, you may see your dog hesitate, but give it a few seconds as he might just be processing the information. Since you are also guiding him with your own hand to the other person's hand, it should be clear that it is the same exercise. If your dog doesn't seem to understand, say "All done," and go back to the two cues again and practice a few more times or take a break and come back after your dog has had some time to take in all this new information before you try again.

Building the Behavior

Now that your dog can target to someone else's hand, you are ready to put it all together. You will need a helper and do this with your dog on-leash in a low level distraction environment in the early stages.

Step 5—Send your dog to "Say Hi"

Instruct your helper to stand about ten feet from you and to ignore your dog as you ask your dog to sit at your side. Use a high rate of reinforcement with your high-value treats as your dog sits by your side. Mark and treat every three to five seconds to make it easy for your dog to Keep Sitting.

Have your helper move toward you slowly, just like when you are walking your dog outside. This is the new component to this exercise. Keep an eye on your dog to make sure he is still able to Keep Sitting as your helper approaches. Remind your helper to stop and take steps away if your dog gets up or even appears that he will get up. If your dog remains seated, have your helper stop five to six feet away from you and ask her to hold her hand in the target position so the moment you instruct your dog to "Say Hi," he can move up to the person. Use your marker to tell your dog he is correct as he touches your helper's hand, and then step back a step or two and feed him at your side. Train four to five times in a number of locations around your home each time you practice. You are looking for your dog to look for the person's hand, "Touch," and turn quickly back to you after you mark so he can get his reward.

Training your dog to have the skills to calmly approach people while on a walk is a benefit to all concerned.

Keep in Mind

This part will go much faster if your helper avoids making eye contact with your dog during practice. At some point you will want your helper to make eye contact and even reach out since these are things that people do in real life. Avoid adding these things until your dog is able to reliably "Say Hi," turn back and be rewarded at your side eight out of ten attempts in several locations.

Raising the Bar

Step 6—Generalize to new people

You will want to generalize this behavior to as many different people as possible so your dog has a clear understanding of the behavior before you take it on the road. Practice with people who are new to the dog both in and outside your house. Look for signs of stress so you don't overwhelm him with people he might not be comfortable approaching.

Keep in Mind

Naturally, if your dog has a history of aggression or reactivity, you do not want to use this exercise with people you do not know. Be cautious with people who you do know, especially with those who might act in a manner that is unpredictable or overwhelming for your dog. Working with a professional positive reinforcement trainer is recommended if you feel any hesitation about doing this exercise.

Step 7—Generalize to new locations and people

As you take this behavior to new locations, you will have to deal with two variables—new locations and new people. The best way to keep this in check is when you see someone who looks interested in your dog, stop them at a distance where you can watch your dog before any interaction. Six to ten feet is a good distance, or far enough away that your dog is unable to jump if that has been a problem. As you hold your hand up in the universal "Stop" signal, smile, and say something like "Hi, my dog is in training, and we are teaching him to greet people in a calm manner. Do you mind if my dog walks up to you so we can practice?" If they agree, continue your conversation by saying, "Will you wait right there? I'm going to have my dog walk to you and touch your hand. If you wouldn't mind, please put your hand out and he will come and say hello by touching his nose to your hand." Be sure to show the person how you would like them to hold their hand before moving forward. This gives you time to watch your dog and see if he is comfortable, rather than having someone rush right up to him, which might end with your dog jumping or other disastrous results.

After you practice what to say a couple of times when people look interested in your dog, it will come naturally and you will be able to take charge of the situation, something your dog will appreciate. Keep your dog's comfort level in mind, and always be willing to go back and practice earlier pieces of the behavior if he seems confused or worried about anything as you work with members of the public. If it seems too much for your dog with that person or in that environment you also should reserve the right to tell people that your dog is not ready just yet, and thank them for trying to help.

With several weeks of practice, this exercise can help your dog relax and behave calmly in public and when greeting new people. People will now just be another target, rather than someone they should jump on when greeting. Your dog and the people you encounter will greatly appreciate this exercise.

Billy moves toward Jake's hand to "Say Hi."

After the "Say Hi," greeting, Billy turns back for his reward.

Problem Solving

When people approach, my dog keeps getting up after I have asked him to sit.

To keep your dog sitting while people approach, you might have to present your reinforcements faster as the person draws nearer, have better treats, or go back to more of the distraction work before adding new people to the exercise. Usually, if you can reinforce faster, and/or with better treats, you can move through this problem quickly. Try doing one to two mark and treats for every step forward your helper takes (having them stop as you reinforce each time) to see if a higher rate of reinforcement will keep your dog focused on you. Take your time and go at your dog's pace so he really gets the idea that sitting and sustaining the sit are the way earn treats and get the person to come forward to visit.

What if helpers or people we approach while practicing don't do what you ask them to do?

As you practice, you will find that people don't always follow your instructions perfectly, and that's okay. Their hand may be too high or too low or they are standing strangely, but it is essential that you don't worry about the other person's presentation. Instead, help your dog do a good job. If your dog doesn't or can't touch their hand, mark for the effort and step back to feed. If you linger there trying to get it right, your dog might decide to engage old behaviors such as jumping.

Exercise 7

The Doorbell Rings—Just a Minute

Does your home seem like the Kentucky Derby every time the doorbell rings as you race your dog to the door? Wouldn't it be wonderful if your dog actually moved away from the door when the doorbell rang rather, than crowd you for position to greet, jump up on, or "eat" the people on the other side of the door? Wouldn't you love to have a dog who knows how to sit, lie down, or even run to another room when the doorbell rings instead of all the embarrassing things your dog currently does? Unfortunately, with many dogs, the doorbell ringing has become a cue for wild and crazy behaviors that so many dog owners suffer with on a daily basis.

Teaching your dog an alternative behavior in this situation is complicated by the fact that there are often three triggering events at work here: (1) the doorbell ringing (or a knock at the door); (2) your verbal response, such as "Just a Minute!" or "Hang On!"; and (3) your movement toward the door. If your dog responds to all three, then your training sessions will have to address each one of these.

This exercise will teach your dog what to do and where to go after the doorbell rings so your guests or delivery people are not accosted by your dog. Rather than hoping your dog will just stop going crazy or wishing you did not have to wrestle your dog away from the door every time you have a visitor, place your bet on a sure thing by training your dog what to do after the doorbell rings. With some effort on your part and a commitment to practicing with your dog, the completion of this doorbell game will make you feel like you just won the Daily Double.

Goals

- Your dog will move away from the door and give you space as you reach for the door.

- Your dog will move to and remain at a designated station while you move to and open the door.

- Your dog can accomplish the above with the added trigger of the doorbell ringing.

Benefits

- Once successfully trained, the doorbell ringing will cue your dog to move away from the door and wait quietly until released.

- By teaching your dog what to do when the doorbell rings (or if someone knocks on the door) you will not only have a calmer dog, your guests will appreciate not being jumped on, barked at, or sniffed in inappropriate areas.

What you will need

- A clicker, or use a verbal marker if you prefer.

- Treats: 20-30 high-value treats per session.

- You may need a six-foot leash with your dog on his regular collar or harness to help him stay in place once you have decided where to send him after the doorbell rings.

- Several people who will ring the doorbell and come into the house as you practice.

Prerequisites

Prerequisites for training this behavior are Keep Sitting and Target to Hand.

Training time

Do ten to fifteen minute sessions at least three to five days a week—at different times during the day to simulate the random times that people show up at the door. A well-trained behavior should be achieved in a couple of weeks if you work on each section as suggested.

Get the Behavior Started

Before you begin, decide where you would like your dog to go and/or what you would like your dog to do after the doorbell rings. If your dog has a history of jumping and behaving like a circus act gone mad when the doorbell rings, your goal might be to send him to another room, to a crate, or outside for simplicity or safety reasons. If your dog just barks or pushes you out of the way to "greet" your guests, you can train a sit or down after the doorbell rings. Your final decision should be one based on safety and realistic expectations. It isn't reasonable to ask a dog that escapes or has a history of nipping or aggressing when guests first arrive to sit or lie down—however, that is achievable for a friendly dog who just gets overly excited.

Reaching out to touch the doorknob is often one of the triggers that sends an already excited dog over the top with anticipation that someone is visiting or is a potential intruder. This being the case, it's important that you first train your dog to calm down and give you space so you can actually walk to the door unencumbered and without a wrestling match. Once you have this component, you can inform your guests that you will be with them in a moment, *just before* you direct your dog what to do, and before actually opening the door.

Step 1—Teach your dog to move away from the door as you reach for the doorknob.

The preliminary step in training this diversion exercise is to teach your dog to move away from the door as you reach for the doorknob, one of the three triggering events. During the early stages of this training, your dog doesn't have to do anything except move away from the door, so don't also ask for a sit or other trained behaviors just yet.

Invite your dog to come with you to the closed front door. If you are using a clicker, place a number of treats in the hand with your clicker (you want the other hand free), take a deep breath, reach out with your empty hand, and touch the doorknob, turning it slowly while you observe your dog. Watch your dog carefully since you will be looking for subtle movements during these early stages. At this point, be sure to not open the door, just jiggle the doorknob.

Let your dog move around freely, but look for any movement away from the door. Use your marker and treat when your dog moves or backs away even the tiniest bit. Mark and treat again once your dog is in a position away from the door, reaching out to feed him so he doesn't have to move toward you to get his treats. Release your dog with "All done" or another release cue. Repeat this several times.

Step 2—Approach the door from different directions

As you practice this, approach the door from several different areas in your home, rewarding your dog for any movement away until you have repeated this eight to ten times. You want to vary your approach to the door so your actions are similar to when you actually go to the door after the bell rings. Be sure to tell your dog "All done" or use another release cue after each successful movement away from the door. Remember to take breaks between your practice sessions.

Continue to practice just holding the doorknob and then marking and treating for movement away from the door. When you see that your dog has figured out that the mark is happening by moving away after you touch the doorknob, you are ready to train the next step.

Keep in Mind

If your dog continues to move toward the door when you reach for the doorknob, you may need to practice these first two steps for many days. The length of time required depends on your dog's history of rushing the door. Take your time teaching this part of the exercise since this is the part that will help your dog stay focused when you do add the doorbell.

Building the Behavior

As noted above, there are up to three triggering events in this scenario. Now you are going to add a verbal cue—"Just a Minute"—as well as reaching for the door. If your dog has a history of associating the words "Just a Minute" with someone at the door, choose another verbal cue like "Hang On" or "I'll Be Right There."

Step 3—Add the verbal cue

Steps 1 and 2 were designed to deal with the trigger of you reaching for the door, and by now your dog should be giving you some space at the door. Once you have achieved that element, add a verbal cue, which tells your dog there is something you want him to do when the doorbell rings. If your dog has a history of reacting to whatever you typically say (assuming you have a habit of doing so), you will need to choose a verbal cue different from what you have said in the past. For the sake of simplicity in this exercise, let's assume that your dog has no history with the cue "Just a minute."

Step 4—Encourage the dog to move to your designated area

Once you have walked to the door, touched the doorknob, and announced the "Just a minute" cue, turn, and move away from the door, encouraging your dog to move with you by using your "touch" cue so you can help him move easily to his place. The goal is to get four to five steps away from the door, then mark and treat several times where you stopped, using your best treats. Then cue your dog to "Sit" (and keep sitting) where you want him to remain (see Step 5). Soon, this will become one fluid movement and you won't need to mark and treat the initial movement from the door, only the final, desired behavior.

Keep in Mind

It is best to use average-value treats as you begin to add movement away from the door, while marking and treating for the initial movement. Switch to high-value rewards once you get your dog to the area where he will be confined or where you want him to be stationed in a sit or down. This will help plant the seed that the best rewards come after he moves away from the door.

Building the Behavior

Step 5—Practice sit or down at designated area.

If you choose to have your dog go to a particular spot and perform a sit or down, make sure he is fluent with that behavior. I also recommend that you have a mat or rug in position for the dog to sit or lie on. (The mat used for Relax on a Mat is perfect.) The mat acts as a visual cue for your dog and makes it much easier for him to find his spot each time, all the while preventing your dog from sliding around if the area has a slippery surface.

I have chosen to have my dog move to his mat when I answer the door.

Step 6—Back away from the dog while he sits or lies down

Direct your dog to the mat or rug right after the "Just a minute" cue, and ask for the sit or down. Then begin to slowly back away so you can observe him as you move toward the door to open it. The goal is to move back to the door again as your dog remains on the mat. You should accomplish the distance from your dog in small pieces, taking one step away and then coming right back to mark and treat him. Next, try two steps, quickly moving back again to mark and treat. Continue to add more steps until your dog can remain at the station and you can get all the way to the door.

As you work on getting the distance, take breaks and resume your training sessions by going to the door from different areas in the house. Continue at this level until you can get all the way back to the door with your dog staying in place.

Step 7—Add opening the door

Once your dog can wait at the station, you will now add opening the door as he remains in position. The sequence should look like this:

- Approach the door from different areas in the house.

- Announce the "Just a minute" cue.

- Direct your dog to his station.

- Walk to the door and jiggle the doorknob.

Did your dog remain in place? If he did, walk all the way back to him to mark and reward, then repeat several times before adding the next step of opening the door.

When you are ready to open the door, open it just a little, close it, and then go back to your dog to mark and reward. Continue until you can open the door completely with your dog remaining in place.

Step 8—Add a "visitor" at the door

Once you are able to open the door entirely, have a helper assist you by waiting outside the door as you open it and have him/her walk in as you go back to your dog to mark and reward.

If your dog gets up at any point, your helper should stop and back up (even going all the way out the door and closing it if needed). You can gently block your dog with your body and direct him back to his station until you can convince him that the way he gets to visit is to continue to sit or lie down.

Practice these components until you can see your dog moving away from the door when you say "Just a minute" and you are successful at directing him back to his station.

If You Need to Confine Your Dog

As noted above, if you cannot trust or train your dog to perform this behavior reliably, and especially if he has a history of getting loose or displaying aggression toward guests, you should confine him rather than having him try to maintain a sit or down. If that is the case, here is what you should do after you say, "Just a minute:"

- Practice getting farther and farther away from the door until you are able to have your dog move to the area where you will confine him.

- When you are ready to confine your dog, you may need to go all the way into the area with him the first few times, so he doesn't think you are "tricking" him into getting locked outside or in another room. This is where the high-value treats will come in.

- Go all the way into the confinement area or all the way outside with your dog (this is another reason you are telling your guests, "Just a minute"), then have a mark and treat party with the high-value rewards! Also, add lots of praise and fun talk at this point. You want your dog to think this is the most wonderful game in the world so when you add the doorbell, it is no big deal and he will head toward the confinement area. You can also do a food confetti party by tossing lots of food around as you leave. After you've successfully trained your dog to automatically go to the confinement area whenever someone comes to the door, you can offer a stuffed Kong or wonderful chew treat as you leave to keep him busy while you go to the door. If you are working with more than one dog, it's important, that you only do this if you know they won't fight over these things.

Raising the Bar

Now we add the third and final triggering event, the sound of the doorbell ringing. Of all the triggers, your dog is most likely to have developed a strong association between hearing that sound and reacting in a way that you do not like! You need to make sure that you have completed the above steps successfully. Your dog should be able to demonstrate the appropriate response to the "Just a minute" cue, i.e., he moves away from the door and goes to the place you have designated for him to wait. Now, what you need to do is pair the verbal cue with the doorbell so he will respond appropriately when the doorbell rings.

Step 9—Without opening the door, pair the doorbell ring with the "Just a minute" cue

Your helper, who is stationed outside, will be the doorbell ringer. You can use cell phones, a walkie-talkie, or a baby monitor to communicate when to ring the bell. After your helper rings the doorbell, walk to the front door, touch the doorknob, and say "Just a minute." Move your dog to the sit/down station or confinement area, and mark and treat when he completes the behavior successfully.

At this point, don't be surprised if your dog regresses a bit as adding the doorbell sound has raised the criteria significantly. Also, don't worry if your dog barks during this phase, especially if he has always barked before when the doorbell rings. In fact you may always have a little barking with the doorbell before your dog moves to the confinement area or his station, but it often becomes limited as he learns what to do. He may also run back to the door as you move away, but hold your ground and wait until he comes back to the area where you stopped and then mark and treat. Be sure to do a number of reinforcements when he comes back to the right spot. Proceed as before with your sessions while ringing the doorbell and not opening the door. Keep repeating these same steps until you can see that the "Just a minute" cue after the bell rings has your dog turning and moving toward his destination.

Step 10—Practice and generalize with new people and opening the door

If your goal is to confine your dog, do so, then go back and invite your helper in after you have your dog in place to simulate someone actually coming in the house. To generalize this to different people, enlist several helpers to assist you with this final stage, and explain that they may have to wait outside a few minutes as you work through this step.

If your dog is training to a station and he is consistently moving there with ease after the bell rings, go back to the steps of just turning the doorknob, and then opening the door a little, and so on—just as you did before the doorbell was added. The only difference is that the doorbell now comes before all the other pieces. Continue until you can open the door and your guest is able to walk past you and your dog.

With continued practice, the constant race to the front door will be eliminated, the doorbell will no longer be like the starting bell of the Kentucky Derby, and of course, your guests will gladly wager that visiting with you results in a big payoff—walking into your home untouched by your dog.

Problem Solving

My dog pushes me and jumps on me when I go to the door and touch the doorknob.

Your dog might be super excited to think someone is at the door or that he is going for a walk when you touch the doorknob. If your dog pushes toward the door or jumps on you, gently step between him and the door using your body to impede his movement, stepping forward into his space if needed to have him slide off of you. Take a deep breath to help him relax. Do not make eye contact or talk, as this often gets dogs more excited. You can calmly take a few steps back from the door if you need to communicate to him that you are not opening the door. Dropping several treats in a row on the floor for your dog to find as he tries to figure out why you are not leaving will help your dog calm down faster since eating helps to calm the excitement, which, in turn, will help your dog "think" again. Just be sure to drop the treats slightly away from the door to give him the picture that good things happen away from the door.

My dog gets up after I have him sit at the station.

If your dog gets up at any point after you stationed him in a sit or down it is important that you do not inadvertently reinforce this behavior. You don't want your dog to learn that he can get up, follow you, or greet people on his own, and still get a reward. Instead, after you have him back in place, smile and use your voice and praise to encourage him to stay put until you have made it all the way back to the location where you or your helper were when he got up. Once you get that far, walk back to your dog, then mark and treat several times. This helps him get the picture that you want him to remain there, and for doing so, you will come back and reward him. If your dog keeps getting up, release your dog and train after he has had a break. When you come back to training, make it easier by only taking a step or two away in the early stages, or just having your helper stand quietly inside the threshold of the door if that is the part where your dog is having the difficulty. In addition, you can temporarily use a leash or tether to prevent your dog from moving too far away from the station until he better understands that sit/down right there is the answer.

I've added the doorbell and my dog doesn't move away from the door.

If, after the doorbell rings, your dog doesn't stay back or move away from the door after you touch the doorknob, drop your standards, and start over again. Simply work on touching the doorknob after the bell rings until you have your dog moving back again. This sometimes happens with dogs who have a strong history of rushing the door when the bell rings. No big deal, just show him that it's the same game he learned earlier, but this time the doorbell rings first. Be sure your dog does this part successfully before moving forward to opening the door.

Exercise 8

GETTING OUT THE LEASH

Many pet parents are familiar with the problem of their dogs bouncing off walls and displaying general rowdiness the minute they pull out their dog's leash. It can often seem like a round of World Class Wrestling just trying to get the leash on prior to heading out for a walk. And then, when you finally do, your dog almost pulls your shoulder out of its socket in his excitement to get out the door (which can be dangerous if there are steps or stairs to negotiate when you step outside!). While your dog's enthusiasm for his walk should be appreciated, going through the hassle of getting started can take away from your enjoyment and leave you with a dog who is overly stimulated by stress hormones, albeit good ones. Not much learning will take place in that state of mind.

The key to helping your dog is to teach him that going out for a walk on-leash begins with him sitting or standing next to you and displaying an acceptable degree of calmness long before the door opens. The dog's task is to exhibit calmness while standing next to you and his reward will be a walk you can both enjoy.

Goals

- Your dog remains calm when you pull out and attach his leash.

- Your dog moves close to you in the reward position in the presence of the leash.

- Your dog actively, but calmly, looks up at you after you have attached his leash while waiting to begin walking.

Benefits

- You can avoid the chaos that many dogs create once they realize that the leash is out and you are going for a walk.

- If you do not have your dog's calm attention after you put the leash on him, you will often not be successful once you venture outside. When your dog learns to relax and be calm while having his leash attached to his collar or harness, you will have a dog who is more aware of your presence and much easier to train as you go forward with leash walking.

What you will need

- A clicker, or use a verbal marker if you prefer.

- Treats: 10-20 high-value treats per session.

- A six-foot leash and your dog on a regular buckle collar, a limited-slip collar, or a harness (a front-clip is preferred if you use a harness as it will give you more control and most large pet supply stores carry one brand or another).

- Comfortable shoes, as you will be moving around a lot during these exercises.

- A quiet, comfortable, indoor place with minimal distractions in which to train.

Prerequisites

Sit and Keep Sitting behaviors are prerequisites for this exercise.

Training time

Be sure you have a solid five to ten minutes of uninterrupted time to devote to this a couple of times per day.

Get the Behavior Started

Step 1—Convince your dog there will be no walk until he is calm

At first, your dog will likely exhibit whatever behavior he usually does as you bring out his leash—common reactions include jumping up on you, barking, or racing toward the door. If this happens, simply place the leash down when your dog behaves wildly and go about your routine for a few minutes without trying to put the leash on him. (Put the leash where he can't get it if he is a leash biter or tugger.) This will show your dog that you won't give him attention when he behaves that way, and in fact, you won't clip on his leash either. Once he settles down, cue "Sit." If he remains seated, mark and reward, moving closer and closer with the leash until he is able to maintain calmness while you clip on the leash.

Step 2—Place food near your foot on the side where you will walk your dog

Once you have your dog on-leash, move to an area where you are going to practice (you should still be in the house with low distractions) and begin by placing a food reward on the floor right next to the outside of your foot. This should be on the side where you would like your dog to walk. Don't ask your dog to do anything at this point, but go ahead and place several treats, one at a time, near your foot so he learns that being close to you in that position is a good thing. Stand all the way up between each treat. It doesn't matter what direction your dog is facing right now; he is learning that being near you is rewarding.

Place a food treat next to your foot on the side where you walk the dog.

When you deliver the food, be sure you are holding it in the hand closest to the dog. It is important that you do not lean over your dog to place the treat down, just bend at the knees, and then slide your hand down near your leg and toward the floor. You will get some exercise in the process! Try to place and not drop the food since you don't want your dog to chase any stray treats. That would be rewarding your dog for leaving you! Move to a couple different places and do a few more repetitions. Then continue the training until you have done it fifteen to twenty times in several different locations.

Building the Behavior

Step 3—Use a marker to reinforce calmness by your side

Steps 1 and 2 have taught your dog that he will be rewarded for remaining calm as the leash is attached to him *and* remaining at your side. Now we want to teach him to add a sit to the process. Cue him to "Sit," then mark and reward, still placing the reward on the ground. Build duration so he can sit calmly for at least several seconds in this position. This will reinforce calmness prior to heading out for a walk.

Step 4—Mark eye contact and your dog seeking you

At this point, your dog should be sitting calmly by your side. Stop placing the treats in front of him for just a moment and see what he does. If he looks up at you to see what is going on, mark the eye contact, but this time feed him from your hand. This will reinforce your dog for paying attention to you, rather than you trying to get his attention all the time. When you feed your dog, do so on the side where you want him to walk, rather than reaching out to him. It's important that he learn his rewards are right next to your leg, which will encourage him to stay closer to you.

If your dog doesn't look up at you, continue with five to ten more treats on the floor, and then wait to see if he looks up at you. By allowing him to take his time and adjust to his environment and then choose to look up at you, you will have a dog who is more steady and attentive as you proceed. Take a break and end the training session.

Raising the Bar

Step 5—Practice going out the door

It's time to practice this behavior beyond the confines of your home. You should proceed very slowly because you want to teach your dog to stay focused on you while being exposed to new distractions. Be sure he has had enough practice so that he sits and makes eye contact with you consistently. If you can't get your dog's attention in his usual environment, you sure won't have it when you leave home, so don't rush him if he is not ready.

This should be your goal: your dog is sitting calmly, looking at you, with a loose-leash, prior to going for a walk.

Begin by asking your dog to sit while on-leash near the door. Move toward the door and open it. If he gets up from the sit, quietly shut the door and block his exit by standing between him and the door. Ask your dog to sit again, and as long as he continues to sit, the door continues to open, but with you between him and the exit.

If your dog is still sitting as the door opens, turn to go out and invite him with you with a cue, like, "Okay," but the second he steps over the threshold, mark it so your dog turns right back to you for the reward. This will teach him that the first thing he should do when walking outside is to check in with you.

Go back in and practice it again so your dog learns to sit when you open the door and to immediately turn to you when he steps outside. Strive for an 80% success rate before moving forward.

If for some reason your dog doesn't turn back when you mark as he goes out the door, go back to placing several treats on the ground near your feet, just like in Step 2, to encourage him to calm himself by sniffing the ground and eating. This also rewards him for staying near you. Drop a few more treats if he still seems distracted and then wait to see if he will check in with you. Once your dog looks up at you, mark and reward from your hand and next to your walking side. If he still is unable to check in with you, go back in and practice Step 2 inside, but with the door open. Move closer and closer to the door until you can see your dog understands this is the same behavior as before, but now there are some distractions.

Step 6—Practice with people and other dogs nearby

Once your dog can go through the door with you in a calm manner consistently, you will be ready to move around more and practice in different areas outside. You want your dog to check in with you no matter where you are. This skill will be the foundation for success with the Exercise 9, Calm Loose-Leash Walking.

Next, arrange to have helpers walk by, then mark and reward your dog for calm behavior. Stay at this level until you can keep your dog's attention when people walk by, and finally, with other dogs being walked by. Be sure to keep your dog and the distractions far enough apart as you begin adding them, so your dog can be successful. Once that happens, you can get closer and closer.

Problem Solving

When I take out my dog's leash, he goes crazy. I have a hard time even getting him on a leash, he is so excited.

If your dog is over the top just seeing the leash, be sure to train the Relax on a Mat exercise to help your dog learn that bringing out a leash, doesn't always mean you are going walking. Also, use pulling out a leash as a distraction when you work on the Keep Sitting exercise.

Exercise 9

CALM LOOSE-LEASH WALKING

Wild and crazy dogs often do not make for pleasant walking companions. Most are notorious pullers, and it is the purpose of this exercise to take a dog who is a pulling fanatic and convince him that walking calmly by your side will be to his advantage. The frustration of having a dog dragging one's body down the street, poop bag in hand, leaves many pet parents feeling as though they are nothing more than glorified pooper scoopers, which is not exactly what most people have in mind when they go out for a walk.

Unfortunately, most dogs like this find pulling quite reinforcing—they usually get their way while you find yourself in the role of an accomplice! If a dog has a strong reinforcement history of pulling on leash, he may find it very difficult to catch on to the idea of not pulling and walking nicely with you despite all of your efforts and money spent on the newest equipment "guaranteed" to prevent your dog from pulling.

To help your dog change this pattern of pulling, you need to teach him that he can still get to his destination if he steps together with you, learns to look and check in with you, maintains the heel position, and walks on a loose-leash. Sounds like a lot to deal with, but actually, these can be fun exercises and games that dogs will love to play and they will help cement your relationship with your dog. That relationship is a key element to mutual loose-leash walking rapport between you and your dog.

This is what walking the dog looks like for too many owners!

A leash is an essential tool when going out in public with your dog. It provides you at least some degree of control over him as you can use it to restrain his movements. However effective it might be, it is cooperation, not restraint that you should seek as you walk your dog.

Loose-leash walking is a skill learned by both humans and dogs, and like any skill, it takes practice, so take your time, plan many training sessions, and don't move on until your dog has a clear understanding of each component that contributes to good leash walking skills.

There are many ways to hold a leash, but the most secure way is to loop the handle of the leash around your thumb or index finger, and then gather the excess in the palm of your hand until you have a nice "U" between you and your dog when he is positioned at your side. How much leash you gather up will depend on the size of your dog. You can also fold the leash at a point where it creates the "U." Loop the fold of leash around your thumb or index finger, and allow the excess leash to dangle if you don't want a lot of bulk in your hand.

By looping the handle or the fold of your leash around your thumb or forefinger and then cupping the rest of your fingers around the part of the leash that drapes across your palm, the leash cannot slip through your hand.

Loop the handle or the fold of your leash around your thumb or index finger as shown here.

Goals

- While on-leash, your dog pays attention to you and you take the first step *together.*

- Your dog learns how to find the heel position before you actually begin walking him.

- Your dog walks on a loose-leash in a heel position even when there are distractions.

Benefits

- You get off to a good start on your walk because he knows how to come into the "Heel" position so you can start together as a team.

- Teaching your dog how to find "Heel" provides him a focus and helps connect the two of you before taking a walk.

- Your dog learns to find his way back to your side if he steps out of position.

- Teaching your dog how to walk calmly and attentively on a loose leash not only benefits your dog with mental and physical exercise, but it saves your shoulders and body in the process.

What you will need

- A clicker, or use a verbal marker if you prefer.

- Treats: 30-50 high-value treats for each session.

- A six-foot leash and your dog on a regular buckle collar, a limited-slip collar, or a harness (a front-clip is preferred if you use a harness as it gives you more control and most large pet supply stores them).

- Something to hold treats that you can get to as you train. A treat bag is ideal, but a fanny pack or a plastic bag clipped to your pocket will also work.

- Comfortable shoes, because you will be moving a lot during these exercises.

Prerequisites

The Eye Contact and Name Recognition behaviors are prerequisites for this exercise.

Training time

Do five to ten minutes each time you practice, at least once or twice a day and three to five days a week if possible. The more you practice, the easier it will be to keep your dog focused, and ultimately, walking nicely on leash. Loose-leash walking can take anywhere from a week to a couple of months depending on your dog, his reinforcement history of pulling, and how often you practice the exercise.

Get the Behavior Started

Each time your dog pulls away from you while on a walk *and* is able to reach his desired destination, he is receiving positive reinforcement. Your goal in this exercise and the lesson you want your dog to learn is that he can still get to his destination, but it is paying attention to you and cooperating with you that will get him there.

Step 1—Get eye contact and step away, mark the first step and movement toward you

Have your dog on a leash and wait until he looks up at you. Since you have already worked on Eye Contact, your dog should be motivated to focus on you. Once he does, take a step away from him. This can and should include stepping backward, stepping to the side, or stepping forward (you will want to mix it up so your dog pays attention). Most dogs will step toward you if you begin to move away. Use your marker the first step your dog makes in your direction, but feed right at your side to reinforce the heel position. If need be, you can and should give your dog encouragement to move toward you by using Name Recognition or patting your leg to help him if he seems stuck or starts to pull away from you.

Step 2—Step away, change direction, and reward at your side

Achieving eye contact with your dog before going on a walk is a great first step.

Now, establish eye contact once more, then step away in a different direction. Watch carefully so you can mark that first step your dog takes toward you. Again, feed at your side. This will show your dog that stepping in your direction results in good things and rewards always happen at your side. Continue doing this five to ten times and then end the training session.

Step 3—Practice in new locations and with increasing distractions

Now practice in several different locations around your home so your dog gets the idea that no matter where you are, the game is the same—sticking by your side is rewarding. At this stage, stay inside alone with your dog since you want to create a strong behavior first and then gradually add more difficult distractions such as going outside, having people in the area where you are working, or even placing a favorite toy on the floor, but out of the reach of your dog.

Keep in Mind

Wrapping the leash around your hand or your wrist is dangerous to you and your dog if you are unable to disentangle yourself, as in a dog fight or if you tripped and were unable to let go. There are many reports of people being dragged by their dogs and suffering minor to severe injuries.

Building the Behavior

If you are getting the impression that there is much more to loose-leash walking than you might have thought, you are correct. The actual walking is the last part of a carefully planned process that first teaches your dog to pay attention, continue to do so (even with distractions), and how to find the heel position.

If you have been consistent about rewarding your dog right next to your leg in your preferred heel position, he should quickly learn the proper position to take to get his reward, which is standing next to you when on his leash. It is very important that *you* make it clear to your dog where the heel position is, and what it actually means, so that when you ask your dog to "heel," he learns to come to your side and line up with his shoulders next to your leg.

Step 4—Lure your dog to the heel position and mark/reward

Begin cueing your dog to sit so he is in front, facing you. Mark and reward him for sitting. Reach out with your food hand, allowing him to sniff the treats that are cupped there, and slowly lure your dog from the sit and begin to move so that he will have to get up, turn, and follow you. You will keep your hand at his nose, while you move it to your side as you walk forward enough steps to lure him next to your leg. Mark as soon as his shoulder is lined up at the side of your leg, then stop and open your hand to feed him right there in position. After the initial reward, you should mark and treat a couple of times as you stand together in the "Heel" position to make the behavior of being at your side stronger. As you do this, you will bring your treat hand back up each time between the marker and the reward, so your dog is now listening for the mark and not staring at the hand with the food.

This set of three photos shows how to lure your dog into the heel position.

Practice this eight to ten times. Once your dog has learned to follow your hand with food, you should be able try it without having to lure him with food and direct him into the heel position using only your hand as a guide, then mark and reward as soon as he is aligned at your side.

Step 5—Add a verbal cue

After your dog can successfully follow your empty hand at least 80% of the time, you can add a verbal cue to this behavior just before luring him with your hand. Some suggestions are, "At My Side," "Over Here," or "Heel." Whichever words you choose, be sure to only say it one time. If your dog doesn't respond to your cue, continue to practice without the cue and try again, making sure the environment is an easy one for him. Go back to the cue after you have practiced some more. After your dog is responding to your cue, practice several times a day and move to at least five new locations within your home each time.

Raising the Bar

Leash walking can be as difficult for the dog as it is for humans. It helps to imagine that loose-leash walking is similar to a couple learning how to ballroom dance. At first, there are a lot of missteps and sore toes, but if they commit to lots and lots of practice of the basic steps, they will eventually be able to do the steps in sequence, and ultimately step in unison to the rhythm of the music. If these dancers didn't take the time to practice the basics over and over again, they would look like people with two left feet. The point is, practice the basics. Teach your dog how to stand with you, how to seek you out, and how to find "Heel" before trying to walk around the block!

Now add more steps to you and your dog stepping together and teach him to move and change directions with you. It's important to show your dog how to stay at your side, but it's equally important to teach him how to move out of your way and turn with you when you change directions. Your dog's "job" should be to stay in step with you even when there is something that he would like to explore.

Step 6—Take steps in different directions and mark the first movements toward you

Use your marker and reinforce your dog for being at your side as a warm-up before you begin moving with him. Begin with taking a step forward and marking just as he starts to move with you, then present the food at the side of your leg. Remember to bring your treat hand up and away from the dog each time after your reinforcement. Take another step backward and mark just as he starts to move and turns around to face you. Next, take another step to the right and mark the first movement toward you. Now take a step to the left (leading off with your left foot). Make sure you don't step on your dog; step slightly in front of him as you begin to turn if he walks on the left (start with your right foot if he walks on that side). With each of these steps, mark his first movement to follow along, remembering to feed at the side of your leg.

Give your dog a break for a few minutes and pet him, play ball, or let him sniff the ground before training again. These little breaks are important for learning as well as for keeping your dog engaged in training.

Step 7—Add several steps to your movement forward

Now that your dog has warmed up, you can add a few steps before you mark. Build up the number of steps gradually. Occasionally go back and practice an easier number of steps as well. It's important that you don't just keep making it harder each time, as your dog is likely to feel more stress and less satisfaction that way.

Step 8—Vary the number of steps and change directions

Now that you are varying the number of steps you take, mix up the direction you are stepping as well. This helps your dog pay attention to your movements and learn to step out of your way when you turn toward him. Practice stepping away from your dog while moving backward a good deal, as you want your dog to be familiar with this as you progress with your training.

Make sure in the early stage of learning this skill that you use a high rate of reinforcement and mark and treat frequently to keep your dog in position rather than letting him resort to pulling. If you give him enough information about where to be and how to walk with you via a strong reinforcement program, you should soon see him choosing to stick with you rather than pulling.

Take many breaks between your practice sessions and train in short segments. Five to ten minutes is a good goal. When you practice with your dog, make many direction changes and keep your communication clear by marking and treating a lot when he is in the correct position. It also helps in the beginning to stop each time you mark and reward so your dog learns to stop when you stop. Practice in 20-30 locations, and try to minimize distractions until you are sure your dog can move with you once you begin to practice beyond the confines of your home and yard.

Step 9—Add distractions and head out on the road

Once your dog is able to pay attention and move with you when you change direction, you can add small distractions and begin walking together outdoors in public places. This should be done in small increments so your dog learns a very important lesson about walking on leash with you: The rest of the world is a "maybe," but you will reward him when he has a loose leash. In other words, pulling will no longer work, but sticking with you not only gets great rewards, it also keeps you moving forward.

It may not seem like a big difference, but loose-leash walking in public is much more difficult than at home.

Distractions can be a toy lying on the ground that you walk by, approaching people, or other dogs. The goal is to keep your dog's focus and attention on you no matter what the distraction might be. The distractions you choose to train around should be decided by the level of attention you have established with your dog so far. You may need to go back inside for a bit if he is unable to handle being outside when you add distractions. Start at a distance far enough from the distraction that your dog can maintain his focus on you. If you are unable to walk past a distraction without him pulling, despite a strong reinforcement rate, you will need better treats or more distance from the distraction. You should try to achieve 80-85% success at this level before adding bigger distractions or getting closer to the one you are working with. In other words, your goal should be to walk past a distraction successfully eight out of ten attempts without your dog pulling. He is, however, allowed to look at the distraction.

Step 10—Make the distractions more challenging

Once you have established that your dog can maintain a loose-leash near a certain level of distraction, make it harder by walking near distractions that he is likely to find more tempting. Reward him for maintaining his position near and focus on you. Again, try to achieve an 80-85% success rate before moving to an even more stimulating environment.

Step 11—Add a verbal movement cue

You will now add a verbal cue to your forward movement or any change in direction. This gives your dog information that something is going to happen so he can watch your body and be successful at following your movements. "Let's Go," "Forward," "Okay," or any other word you would like as your cue will tell your dog that you are going to move forward or change directions. Be sure to use the word one time only so your dog associates the word with the movement. If you keep saying it over and over, he may choose to ignore you.

Keep in Mind

It takes lots of practice to obtain good leash walking skills, so commit to *not* moving forward if your dog is pulling and practice, practice, practice! Don't worry about your dog not getting his daily walk for exercise. You will find that you will be taking just as many steps teaching him how to move and turn with you as you would going around the block. You will also get the extra bonus of your dog getting lots of mental exercise during your training. Most pet parents report that their dogs are much more tired after doing this kind of controlled leash walking than when they pulled mindlessly all the way around the block.

Problem Solving

My dog doesn't come up to my side to get the treat, and it seems like he doesn't understand where he should be.

Showing your dog the correct feeding position will usually solve this problem. You should be feeding your dog near where the seam of your pants is located, on the outside of your thigh (lower for smaller dogs). Make it a point to practice this without your dog a number of times, as the position of the reward will "tell" him where you want him to be and you should be well rehearsed before adding him. If you reach out, or reach behind to your dog to reward him, you are "telling" him to stay away from you. Also, remember to bring your hand back up to your stomach or hip every time after you reward your dog so he will learn to listen for your marker and not watch your hand. If he is having a hard time with this, mark any movement toward you, then extend the food toward him, but don't allow him to eat it yet. Guide him with the food to the correct position and then feed him.

My dog walks nicely for a few steps, then pulls. I keep getting him back into position and mark the correct position and treat, but then he pulls again. It seems like I'm training him to pull.

When dogs repeat behaviors, they are doing so because there is a payoff. In this case, your dog has learned that pulling will make you get him back in position and then he gets a treat. Smart dog!

To fix this, when your dog gets back into position, he needs to understand that staying there will get even more rewards. Make a direction change, using your voice to encourage him along, and when you start to move forward again, do multiple marks and treats now that he is back in place and going forward again. Your job is to notice when the dog is getting out of position before he begins to pull. That is when you need to change directions, use your movement cue, and keep his attention.

My dog does fine in the house or the back yard, but once we get off my property it's sled dog all over again.

Many dogs lose their minds the second they walk into the big world—and unfortunately when your dog is that aroused, not much learning can take place. This is an issue of the behavior not being strong enough before exposing the dog a distracting environment. Rather than trying to go for a walk after such a great success in the backyard, commit to training one or two calm steps just outside the front door. Go back to standing with your dog on-leash and reinforcing for Eye Contact. Don't worry about going for the walk, just go back to building the foundation of being able to pay attention to you in that one spot. Once you are getting more focus from your dog, take a break, then come back to that spot and train again. Raise your criteria slowly. If you train as though he has never done these exercises before and train him well before moving from that spot, you should see marked progress. When you think your dog is doing better, proceed with teaching him to walk with you. Consider using better treats and/or use a faster rate of reinforcement to keep your dog's attention if behaviors begin to fall apart.

My dog continues to pull on the leash no matter what I do.

As mentioned above, pulling can be a very hard behavior to extinguish, especially if your dog has been doing it for months or years. To give yourself your best chance of success:

- Watch your dog at all times and try to get him back in alignment with you before he actually hits the end of the leash. You have to really pay attention and then decide which action to take.

- Don't pull on the leash to get your dog back into position. This just gets him used to a tight, rather than loose, leash.

- The Name Recognition behavior is key. If you have mastered that exercise and your dog responds immediately to his name by turning and looking at you, it is much easier to get him back to the proper position.

- Another effective technique is to use your movement cue after calling his name, then immediately move in a different direction and mark and treat once he reaches the heel position.

Harley stepped ahead of Jessica, so Jessica begins to move back and away from where Harley wanted to go. As soon as Harley has caught up with Jessica, she will be marked and rewarded.

- If none of the above techniques work and your dog doesn't respond as soon as you turn, you may have to use gentle leash pressure while moving away from your dog. It's important when you do this to lower your leash hand slightly so it is parallel with your dog's collar or harness and takes the strain off his neck. You may need to bend at the knees to get your hand low enough if your dog is smaller. When you have to use the leash to guide your dog away from a distraction, be sure that you don't tug or jerk on the leash—it can be painful and he is not learning what he is supposed to do. Be sure to mark and reward when your dog starts to move with you.

Jessica lowers the leash with her hand and uses gentle leash pressure to get Jack moving after he got so involved in the environment that he was no longer paying attention.

EXERCISE 10

KEEP CALM WHILE BEING HANDLED

With the exception of the Say Hi behavior, which involves only limited physical contact between your dog and other people, we have been focusing on creating calmness in situations that primarily involve just you and your dog. Training your dog to keep calm while being touched and handled by other people can represent one of the most challenging behavioral problems that dog owners and trainers face. This is especially difficult with dogs who show undue sensitivity to such contact even from their owners. A negative experience on a visit to a veterinarian or a groomer, not to mention a bad run-in with a neighbor, can make it difficult for a dog to learn to be relaxed and calm when faced with having to be handled by someone other than his owner.

Dogs react to these situations in a variety of ways, including barking, lashing out at people, nipping and grabbing clothes, and jumping up on people. Fortunately, most dogs will give off signals before they react overtly, giving you some time to intervene. If your dog displays any of the following signals when being handled or about to be handled, then it's time get proactive and put a desensitization training program in place. These include:

- Apprehension (whining is a typical example)

- Backing away

- Cowering

Regardless of why or how a dog builds a sensitivity to handling (or anything else), it's always alarming when your normally sweet dog all of a sudden struggles, gets wild, pulls or runs away, growls or even snaps during the course of handling, grooming, or petting. No matter how upsetting, it is important to respond and not overreact. If he has resorted to using one of these stronger statements, you can be sure that communication has broken down somewhere along the line and it's time to get busy rebuilding your relationship. If you feel your dog has gone "over the top" and is biting, you should contact a qualified behavior and training consultant to help you. (See Resources.)

Even if your dog has had a steady course of positive experiences with handling, it is always beneficial to add more handling and touching activities to your dog's world, if for no other reason than to offset potential negative experiences in the future. Your veterinarian and groomer will appreciate this, for sure.

Calm Collar Handling or Restraint Exercise

This exercise teaches your dog how to be comfortable when you or someone else takes his collar, and will make it easier for you to move him by his collar even when he is excited or worried.

People need to move or restrain their dogs by the collar for many reasons, including those related to safety. Some dogs accept this type of handling well, but many dogs don't and, some become reactive once their collars are grabbed. That's why it is important to teach your dog that sometimes he will have to be moved or restrained by his collar, and rather than it being a problem, it's simply another opportunity for reward.

The following exercise will help your dog learn that collar handling results in a reward and your attention—the best reward of all!

Goals

- Your dog stays calm and doesn't struggle when you or someone else takes hold of his collar.

- You are able to fade the use of treats over time while training this behavior.

- Your dog is able to perform well in new areas and with distractions.

Benefits

- Many people have been bitten by their own dogs when trying to restrain them by the collar. This can happen when dogs are overly excited, fearful, or aroused by things in their environment. This exercise raises the safety factor and helps your dog be more relaxed when you or someone else has to take hold of his collar.

- Your dog learns to accept collar handling not only by you, but by other people as well. This makes going to the vet or a groomer less stressful for many dogs.

What you will need

- A clicker, or use a verbal marker if you prefer.

- A place to tether or crate your dog where he is able to watch you set up for this exercise.

- Treats: 30-50 medium to high-value treats.

- A six-foot leash and a harness or regular collar.

- A quiet, comfortable, indoor place with minimal distractions in which to train. You will train in different locations with more distractions later.

- A helper or two who will be willing to practice this exercise so your dog learns that other people touching his collar is equally rewarding.

Prerequisites

Sit is a prerequisite for this exercise.

Training time

Do two, five to ten minute training sessions a day, at least five days a week. A well-trained behavior should be achieved in just a couple of weeks.

Get the Behavior Started

Step 1—Set up the exercise

Before you begin, tether your dog, have someone hold him, or place him in a crate where he can watch you as you set this up. Your job is to make a really big deal out of setting little piles of yummy food (three to five treats in each one) in five to ten locations on the floor (spread these out about four feet apart) as your dog watches. He should be getting pretty excited watching you, especially if you are rather animated about the process and talking it up as you place the food down. Have a few additional treats with you in a pocket or a treat bag to reinforce calmness as you train.

Step 2—Guide your dog by the collar to the treats

After you have your piles of treats ready, walk over and take your dog by the collar. He is likely to be so focused on the treats at this point that he might not notice that you are holding the collar—which is a good thing. Gently guide your dog by the collar to the first pile of treats, and allow him to eat them, maintaining your hold on his collar as he does so. (If you have a tiny dog, you can do this up on a table or platform of some sort so you don't have to bend over.)

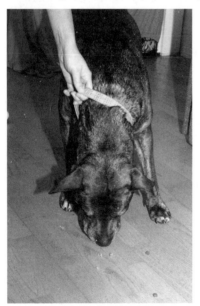

Gently guide your dog by the collar to each pile of treats.

If at any time your dog is squirming to get away from you, take a few deep breaths and keep holding his collar. See if you are able to get his attention by saying his name or using a kissy sound. As soon as he responds to you, softly praise and pop a couple of high-value treats into his mouth until you feel him start to relax. It's important to wait until your dog stops wiggling, even just a small amount, before moving to the treats on the floor because you want your dog to learn that it's calmness that will allow him to get the next pile of food—not squirming. It's also imperative that you guide him to the treats the second he stops struggling so he doesn't become frustrated by the handling. You can build on more calmness as you move ahead with this, but the first few times it's better to respond to the tiniest bit of calm and move him to a pile of treats.

As soon as he is done with one pile, lead him to the next pile, continuing until all of the piles are gone, as long as he doesn't struggle. Stop and help him calm down if he does try to get loose. Be sure to release him with a release cue such as "All done" after he has finished the last pile. Practice this five to ten times over a couple of days before moving to Step 3.

Building the Behavior

Step 3—Sit before moving to each pile of treats

When you can see that your dog can be led calmly from one treat pile to another, you will make the next session more challenging. You will put out just three piles of very low-value treats (like dry kibble) and increase the distance between them up to ten feet. Take your dog's collar, but before moving with him, cue him to "Sit." As soon as he does, mark and reward from your hand with a higher-value reward. If you are using a clicker, be sure not to click with the hand holding your dog's collar as that is too close to his ear.

Take your dog's collar and cue a "Sit" before leading him to the treats.

Once your dog has sat, say a movement cue, such as, "Let's go," and guide him to the pile of treats. Once the pile is gone, cue him to "Sit" once again, then mark and use the high value treats if he does it willingly and calmly. Use the movement cue and take your dog to the next pile, asking for the sit again, then take a break. Stay at this level until you have done this five to ten times over a few days. Try to use different areas of your home each time so your dog can begin to generalize this behavior. Remember you are holding his collar through the entire step. Try taking his collar without saying, "Sit," to see if he has made the association.

Step 4—Reduce the number of piles on the floor

Reduce the number of piles of treats set up on the floor from three to one. Repeat Step 3, reducing the number of treat piles each time. Cue the dog to "Sit" each time you take your dog's collar and then mark and reward. At this point your dog should automatically offer a sit whenever you take his collar since he has learned to associate these behaviors and anticipates being rewarded.

When you have achieved that, reward from your hand as you take your dog's collar and he sits. You no longer need the food on the floor. Use your movement cue and move him a few steps. Always use your movement cue when you want to take your dog by the collar and move him, so he is not caught off guard. Then mark and reward after the movement with high value treats.

Raising the Bar

Step 5—Practice in new areas

Repeat Step 4 at least two times a day, but now train your dog in at least five different areas. Include training in areas where you are likely to need to grab his collar in the future, including near doors or in your garage as you approach your car. Make sure he is continuing to sit as you take hold of his collar. Repeat previous steps as necessary if he regresses.

Step 6—Add distractions

Add some distractions, such as people walking past, or a ball rolling by, and be ready to reward your dog for sitting next to you, and not for straining when you take his collar. Be sure to keep the distractions low enough or far enough away that your dog is able to stay focused on you. Once he is able to sit and relax eight out of ten times with low-level distractions, you can bring the same distractions closer and work toward that same goal.

This will make staying with you much more fun than trying to get to something while straining forward. Stay at this level until your dog is relaxing when you take his collar during bigger distractions, such as the door opening. If you do this every day for the next couple of weeks, your dog will look forward to having his collar handled and touched.

Step 7—Reduce the food

You do not always want to have to reward you dog every time he calmly sits when you take his collar. Begin to substitute praise some of the time when he performs correctly. You will still need to reward with treats from time to time, but you should be able to mix the two effectively. Try skipping the treats twice in a row and then go back to treats. Praise every time, but only use treats randomly. This will teach your dog to keep working with you, in hopes that the next time you take his collar and cue "Sit," he might be rewarded. Don't try to fade the food too quickly, especially if your dog has a strong history of misbehaving when people take his collar. Be sure to vary your rate of reinforcement so it isn't getting harder all the time.

Step 8—Have other people take your dog's collar

Now it is time to have your dog learn that it's the same game, even if someone else takes him by the collar. This is such a beneficial skill for your dog to learn since there are many occasions where dogs must be handled by their collars. Examples are vet visits, grooming, or your dog escaping, it's important that he is comfortable with complete strangers taking him by his collar.

Start at the beginning with Step 1 and direct your helper through the entire process even if it goes rapidly. Just because your dog completed the whole exercise with you, that won't necessarily translate to your helper, so help your dog succeed by starting from scratch as though he has never done this before.

If your veterinarian or groomer will cooperate, ask if you can bring your dog in to practice with them taking his collar. Only do this once you have practiced with a few people in your home first. This is great for dogs who are anxious in these environments or around the people who work in these professions because they will get a positive experience and learn that nothing bad happens. They get to practice and go home; no grooming, no shots, etcetera.

Continue working with different people taking your dog's collar until you are able to fade the food to a minimum with them as well. If your dog is still uncomfortable around strangers do not do this exercise without the help and instruction of a professional behavior and training expert to guide you.

Exercise 11

Accepting Restraint

This exercise teaches your dog how to be comfortable and accept restraint when you or others need or want to handle him. The benefits of your dog accepting touch or being handled by others is obvious, but some owners even have difficulties in this regard with their own dogs. It feels so personal when a dog does not like to be held or restrained. Scientists and counselors alike have expounded the health and emotional benefits of touching a dog, so if your dog is reserved about being touched or groomed, it certainly can seem like rejection.

While working on this exercise, keep the ABC warning signs—Apprehension, Backing away, Cowering—in mind as you watch your dog for signs of stress and discomfort as you proceed. Training should proceed only when he appears relaxed and comfortable so he can learn that touching is a wonderful thing and that he will not die if he is held or his feet or face are touched.

Goals

- Your dog stays calm when he is sitting next to you while you are touching him.

- Your dog learns to be comfortable being held, picked up, and restrained.

Benefits

- There are both short and long-term benefits to teaching your dog to accept restraint. The most obvious is that you will be able to hold your dog without sending him into frenzy, and that he will be able to relax when you or someone else needs to look at a paw, brush his fur, or examine his body.

- Easier vet and grooming visits.

- Avoiding extra charges for medication or surcharges for extra time to handle your dog.

What you will need

- Your dog's "relax mat" and a brush if you are working on grooming.

- Treats: 50-100 medium to high-value treats.

- A six-foot leash and a harness or regular collar.

- Since you will use both hands during this exercise, a regular box clicker can be difficult to handle and will likely be too loud for use near your dog's ear. While you might be able to find a smaller, quieter clicker like an I-Click, it may be easier to use a marker word or a tongue click if you feel that trying to coordinate the exercise and the clicker is too much. (See Resources for where to get I-Clicks.)

- A quiet, comfortable, indoor place with minimal distractions in which to train. You will be working on the floor with your dog, so find a comfortable spot for yourself as well. Have a table accessible that you can lift your dog onto to simulate a vet or groomer visit, especially if your dog has had difficulty in these situations.

- Some helpers to touch/handle your dog.

Prerequisites

You should have practiced the "Relax on a Mat" exercise before moving to this exercise. Having that skill helps your dog be more comfortable in the early stages of this training since he will have learned to relax when he sees his mat.

Training time

Do five to ten minute sessions twice a day if possible, at least three to five days a week. Your dog will be calmer about being touched, handled, or brushed in just a few sessions, but you have to build up to the more difficult areas on your dog's body and that can take several weeks or even months.

Get the Behavior Started

While this exercise is designed to teach your dog to accept gentle restraint, you may need to begin your training with something as seemingly easy as having your dog remain calm while being close to you. If your dog can handle that you can skip to Step 4.

Step 1—Reward for coming close and calmness on his mat near you

Sit on a chair near your dog, and begin by dropping the food when he lies down on his mat. This will reinforce him for coming in close and being calm. Don't try to touch him just yet. You are only reinforcing your dog for being close to you for the time being. Do about eight to ten treat drops at this step before moving on.

Step 2—Sit next to your dog and reward tolerance of you being in his space

Look for your dog to be on his hip (or splay-legged) and relaxed. Once you see that, you should sit on the floor right next to the mat and drop treats again. Since you are changing the picture for your dog by sitting on the floor, you may have to go back to rewarding faster to help him realize that you are doing the same "Relax on a Mat" exercise, just with you sitting right next to him. This builds tolerance of being near you on the floor—a challenge for many dogs. Again, don't try to touch your dog just yet. If he is doing well with you sitting next to him, begin to slow your rate of reinforcement before you release him for a little break by saying your release cue and picking up the mat. This will give him time to process this experience prior to moving to the next step.

Step 3—Add a marker and soft praise

When you come back to work on the next part of this exercise, add a marker signal. As mentioned above, it might be easier to use a marker word rather than a clicker. Sit down next to your dog and mark/reward continued calmness. Praise him while he eats—this will help create a strong association of your voice, calmness, and good things. Your soft praise after the marker will also help to soothe your dog.

Step 4—Add touching

You are now ready to add touching your dog to the training. Always initiate touching your dog's body in a place that is the least sensitive, and as you progress, you will slowly move toward the area where he has shown more concern. In addition, be careful to not reach over the top of your dog's head or lean over him. That would put added pressure on him, making it more difficult to desensitize him. If he is particularly sensitive to being touched or handled, you may need to undertake a desensitization training session (see page 161).

If your dog reacts calmly to your touch, mark and reward. Don't rush this part, especially if he has shown any of the ABCs during past handling and touching. Start out next to your dog on the mat, but you may find it more comfortable to have your dog up higher on a piece of furniture where you can reach him better. Or, you can sit in a chair and work on a bigger dog while he is on the floor.

This dog is being rewarded for sitting calmly while being handled.

What a Desensitizing Training Session Might Look Like

• If your dog is sensitive around his feet, start at the top of his leg. If he is sensitive around his head, start at his back end, and so on.

• Sensitive paws will be the example—you will start with your hand coming near the top of your dog's front leg at the same time the treat is coming near his mouth. Use a verbal mark or clicker, rewarding while maintaining your hand on his leg.

• Your touch should be very light and last just long enough for your dog to finish his treat, then remove your hand. Quiet praise is fine after the marker.

• Stay at this level for ten to fifteen repetitions and then move down his leg an inch at a time, using your marker, and then feeding and touching all at the same time. Look to get about the same number of repetitions before moving forward.

• If at any point your dog pulls his leg or foot away, say your release cue and stop for a moment. Your dog should be disappointed that you stopped and should be more cooperative when you resume. Start at the top of the leg again and work your way down until you can get all the way to the foot. If you are still having trouble, try a higher-value food reward.

• After you have worked your way down your dog's leg and to his paw with that very light touch, go back to the top again. This time you will maintain your touch slightly longer, then follow with your marker, the food, and your praise. This should have your dog making the association that touch equals a marker, your praise, and the treat.

• Move all the way down the leg again with light touch and give your dog a ten minute break.

• When you come back to work on this next part, start at the beginning again with the simultaneous touch on the opposite leg from where you began, and work your way down in the same manner as the first leg.

• Take many little breaks and always be willing to stop and go back to the easier level if your dog displays any of the ABC reactions.

• After you have completed both legs, you can start to add pressure to your touch. Begin at the top of the leg again, but put your hand around your dog's leg and apply slight pressure for as long as it takes him to eat the treat, using your marker and feeding simultaneously. Be sure to add your praise as you do this. It also helps to take deep breaths as you work to mirror calmness to him.

• Move all the way down the leg with a light pressure hold, then move back up to the top and start over. Now, however, after you mark, release your hold and then feed and praise your dog.

• Go as slow or as quickly as your dog allows, and remember to take many breaks between sessions. Keep in mind there is no set time for how long this will take. The goal is for your dog to learn to be more comfortable with accepting touch in sensitive areas.

• Once you have worked on the spots where your dog is sensitive to touch or handling, do this same process all over his body so he gets the same rewards for the less sensitive areas on his body as well. That will help him feel better about being touched, since the focus won't always be the sensitive areas. Practice this several times a day for two to three minutes each time and in different locations around your home so your dog is comfortable with handing and touching in different environments.

Building the Behavior

Step 5—Reward while lightly draping your arm over your dog's back

After you have completed sitting near your dog and the above touching exercises for several sessions (some dogs will need a few days), you can then begin adding body restraint if that is your goal or your dog needs work in this area. You will begin the same as before by putting down your mat and offering some treats as your dog comes over and lies down. Sit on the floor next to your dog so you are both facing the same direction. Begin with a light touch over your dog's back (like draping your arm over someone's shoulders or, if your dog is small, use your hand over his body). If he remains calm, use your marker and praise while giving the treat between his feet, then removing your arm as he finishes his reward. After you have done a number of repetitions on one side, change, and do the other.

Step 6—Apply light pressure and hold for a few seconds

Complete ten to fifteen repetitions of just draping your arm over your dog before you shift to actually holding your dog for a couple of seconds at a time. With your arm draped over your dog, put gentle pressure on him by placing your open hand on his side and applying light pressure as though you were trying to move him closer to you. Keep in mind this is a very gentle touch. You will do ten to fifteen repetitions at this level, and if all seems well, add a little more time (one to two seconds), without increasing the pressure before you reward.

Drape your arm over the dog and apply light pressure. As can be seen here, your dog may show some anxiety about this at first.

Keep in Mind

At this point, your praise and the food reward should be paired together but, going forward, you are going to change things a little with your marker and your praise. Now that you are adding more time before you let your dog go, you want a way to help him understand that the marker is coming (along with the reward), since it is not going to happen as quickly as in past sessions. You will now use praise as a way to assure your dog that his reward is forthcoming— like "cheerleading" or "coaching" your dog. You can say something like, "Good boy, that's a good boy," as a way to help him understand that he is on the right track and to keep him interested and calm until you use your marker and the reward is presented.

It's essential that you go slowly with this part, especially if your dog is uncomfortable with restraint or has had a bad experience while being restrained in the past. Ideally, you will progress through this gradually enough that your dog doesn't notice that you are holding him. However, if your dog struggles at any point, release him and say "All done," pick up the mat, and end the training for a short time before trying again (30 seconds to a minute later). You want your dog to understand that you will stop if he is uncomfortable, but you will also stop giving him rewards, interaction and praise, so it is his choice. If you work up to the restraint slowly using lots of reinforcement, your dog should not be struggling when you do add more time to your hold.

Step 7—Hold different parts of the dog's body

Is all going well? If so, move your arm position to different parts of your dog's body, including around his neck, with this slight pressure hold. Take your time on this—take several days or even weeks if your dog is exceptionally sensitive or worried about restraint. The goal is to help him become comfortable with holding and/or restraint, and skipping steps or rushing could set you back.

Raising the Bar

There are three parts to this section: (1) Picking up and holding your dog; (2) Helping your dog tolerate grooming; and (3) Helping your dog accept *other people* touching, handling, or grooming him. Assuming your dog does have issues with being handled, you should start with Part 1 and move on in sequence to Parts 2 and 3 if they are relevant to your dog.

Part 1—Picking Up and Holding Your Dog

Step 8—Practice slight lifts with your dog's feet still on the ground

If your final goal is to be able to hold your dog in your lap or pick him up for whatever reason, you will next to do slight lifts using the same arm drape as before. Drape your arm over your dog, but this time reach under his chest and apply just enough pressure to lift him slightly but at the same time keeping his feet on the ground. You may need to support his belly area with your other hand if your dog is big, and you may need to stand up. Position yourself so you feel comfortable, but are not leaning over your dog's head. You don't want him to feel off balance, since you have worked so hard to get him to accept your hands on his body. Lift your dog slightly and then release the pressure. If you can do this successfully, use your marker, reward and praise, removing your hand completely each time so he has time to process. This slight lift should be very quick and followed with your marker, the treat, and praise. Stay at this level for ten to fifteen repetitions before moving on to lifting your dog off the ground.

By the way, your dog is allowed to "leave" at any time. Let him move away from you if he chooses to, but don't give up—he might just be thinking about things and be willing to try again in a matter of seconds. If he doesn't return within a minute, say your release cue and pick up the mat.

Step 9—Lift your dog so his feet leave the ground

If your dog seems okay and stays with you after the slight lift, move ahead to lifting so his feet leave the ground. Progress by doing a little more each time until you can place him in your lap, hold him in your arms or place him on a table or other piece of furniture. After your dog is in your lap, in your arms, or up on something, praise and do multiple treats in a row so he understands that being there *really* pays off. Don't force this part—allow your dog to get down, or move from your lap after just a couple of seconds, but stop giving the rewards once he is back on his mat. If you were able to hold or have your dog in your lap for several repetitions, give him a break. Release him, end the session, and pick up the mat.

Keep in Mind

You can test how effective your training is by sitting on the floor without the mat and waiting to see if your dog comes over to you on his own as if he would like to do this again. If this is the case, get the mat and do a couple more little sessions, but keep it short so your dog doesn't get too full or become bored with too much training.

Step 10—Add more time

As you progress in subsequent training sessions of holding your dog or lifting him to a piece of furniture, add more time to this exercise. Hold back your marker, reward, and praise until you get a little more time, working up to several minutes of calmness before you reward your dog. You can use some quiet encouragement as you build toward more duration and the delay of your marker. Don't be hurried as you add this extra time. You will not want to leap from a couple of seconds to a few minutes, as that would be difficult for most dogs and you might have to start all over again. Rather, build up to the duration by adding few seconds at a time and by doing some short sessions in-between so your dog gets rewarded for easier parts as you work toward the longer periods.

Part 2—Helping your Dog Tolerate (Enjoy?!) Grooming

Step 11—Touching with a grooming tool

If grooming is a problem, it is important that you complete the previous section in its entirety before moving to this part. Your dog should be comfortable with overall touching and handling before adding grooming equipment. Once that is completed, you should begin touching your dog with a grooming tool (start with a brush or comb) on the least sensitive area of his body, then use your marker, reward and praise all at the same time if he remains calm. When your dog is done eating, remove the tool. The goal is to be able to have your dog accept the feel of the brush or comb without actually using them just yet. If he seems overly concerned with the brush you can turn it over—touch him with the backside of the brush to make it easier. Continue using the grooming equipment to touch your dog while simultaneously using your marker and the reward, followed by praise, all the while moving toward more sensitive areas. Be sure to take many breaks so your dog can process what you are doing. Use a release cue such as "All done" to allow your dog to leave until you are ready to train again.

When you have successfully touched your dog with the equipment in his sensitive areas, you are ready to move forward. He should be calm with minimal pulling away as you touch him with the equipment before moving to the next step.

If your dog seems overly concerned with the brush you can turn it over—touch him with the backside of the brush to make it easier.

Keep in mind

If your dog is not comfortable with the tools in one area, you need to step back a bit and go slower toward that area until you can see that he is ready for the next location. Take your time and stay with the easier areas if he seems anxious or is showing any of the ABC signs.

Step 12—Begin to use the grooming equipment

If you feel your dog is ready, you will then begin to do a tiny amount of brushing, combing, or perhaps even nail trimming. Once again, mark and reward, followed with praise as you pull the brush through an inch or two of your dog's fur. Take it slow and make it worth your dog's effort to stay with you during this process. If your dog seems worried, take it back a step and turn the brush upside-down and slide it over the area, working back up to using the bristles.

In the case of nail trimming, you will just make the clipping sound around your dog's paws rather than trying to cut them right away. Your dog will have to be comfortable with the paw hold first, the sound of the clippers near his nails second, and finally one at a time you will trim just the very tip of a nail. Take a break between each nail—even a day or two if needed. The paws are very sensitive areas for dogs, so the slower you go the better. Don't be afraid to stay longer at any step of this training if your dog needs more time. Again, the goal is to get your dog to be comfortable and calm about having his nails trimmed.

Step 13—Begin to work with a hair dryer

Bring in a piece of equipment that makes noise such as a hair dryer. While you may not need to ever touch the dog with a hair dryer, the sights and sounds associated with it can cause a dog concern. I recommend you move the dryer around the dog without turning it on first, marking and rewarding as above, then turning the dryer on.

Part 3—Help your dog accept touching, handling, or grooming by other people

Often when dogs resist others touching or grooming them, it is because they have had a traumatic experience. Veterinary exams, shots, and rough handling by techs or groomers can leave deep emotional scars that may take a good deal of time and effort to overcome. This may be a challenge, but it is worth doing as your dog will be happier and so will the people who need to handle him in the future.

If your dog has growled, snapped, or bitten anyone during handling or grooming, you should work with a professional behavior and training expert who uses positive methods that can help him without risking someone being bitten. On the other hand, if your dog is a wiggle worm, gets worked up, or shows only mild anxiety, you may be able to help him become more tolerant by doing these exercises on your own. You will need to gauge your dog's comfort level with someone touching him before you begin.

As you probably know, you won't always be with your dog when he needs to be touched, handled, or groomed; however, the more you practice with willing helpers, the easier it will be for your dog to accept the touch of others, even when you can't be present.

Step 14—Get your dog to be more relaxed when other people touch him

To begin this process, you will go through all the previous touching and handling steps from Part 1, but you will be marking, rewarding, and praising your dog while a helper does the handling. This helps your dog understand that you approve of others doing these things, as evidenced by your marker and rewards. This also keeps the timing consistent as you can't expect others to know what to mark and when. Proceed slowly and be willing to stop if you see any of the ABC warning signs.

Step 15—Practice with someone else acting as a groomer.

As in Step 14, simply go through all the steps from Part 1, but with someone else doing the grooming. You may actually be able to get a professional groomer to do this if you are a client or a potential client. Once again, proceed slowly and be willing to stop if you see any of the ABC warning signs.

Problem Solving

My dog pulls away from restraint.

Release your dog, pick up the mat, and put your food rewards away. Take a short break. Then come back, but go slower this time, use a lighter touch, better treats, and less duration during the hold.

My dog is squirming to get out of my hands when I hold him.

If all goes well to the point of picking your dog up, but when he is in your arms he begins to struggle, take a few deep breaths and hold him close to your body until you feel him start to be still. It's important to wait until your dog stops wiggling for at least a short time before putting him down so you don't reinforce him for struggling. Make a note to do less training the next time you practice, or do more repetitions at an easier level so he doesn't have to struggle at all. Continue to work on this until your dog is practically jumping in your lap or your arms, or enjoys being picked up and/or held. It is easier for some dogs and they feel more secure if you are sitting, so you might try sitting down with your dog in your arms. If you believe your dog might nip or bite during this process, you should discontinue this exercise and contact a trainer or behavior consultant who can help you.

My dog gets overly active or jumpy when I sit on the ground with him.

Say your release cue, pick up the mat, and give your dog a break for a few minutes. When you come back, have higher-value food rewards to keep your dog's focus on the exercise and not on you. If he starts to get wild when you are next to him, quietly and without talking to or touching him, stand up and take a deep breath. As soon as he relaxes on the mat again, reward him. After your dog is lying on the mat once more, sit back down, and reward quickly between his paws. This might take a couple times, but most dogs will quickly understand that they should be calm, even if you are sitting with them.

Sitting on the floor is physically too difficult for me.

If sitting on the floor is difficult for you, sit on a small stool that brings you closer to your dog, or you can place your dog's mat on a couch and have your dog come up there. You may also have to lower your expectations a little since doing "Relax on a Mat" on the couch might be new to him. Go back to rewarding sitting if he doesn't understand to lie down on the couch. However, he should get the idea quickly if you have trained "Relax on a Mat" thoroughly.

My dog pulls away or leaves when he sees grooming tools, so I can't get started with this part.

This is not uncommon if your dog has had a bad experience with grooming. This means you will begin a little differently with him when introducing the grooming tools. Rather than trying to touch your dog with the tool, simply show him the tool. If he stays in place, use your marker and feed while praising him for looking at it and remaining in place. If your dog moves away, hold the tool farther away the next time so he can see it, but still feel safe about you holding it. Take it slow. You should do ten to fifteen repetitions at each level, moving a few inches closer with the tool as you begin each new training session. Keep your sessions fun (remember to smile, praise, and breathe) as you go forward. Take short breaks between each session and be willing to spend more time at an easier level if your dog is moving away when you get closer. Remember to use very high-value rewards.

FINAL THOUGHTS

As you begin to understand more about your dog and make changes in the way you live and train with him, you will begin to appreciate that he is an individual with a unique personality. That is the true beauty of living with a dog.

Even on those days when things are not going the way you had hoped, remember to breathe and consider life from your dog's point of view. You may just find some humor in the situation, as dogs are truly the comics of the world. Enjoy your dog for what he is—a dog! There is poetry, music, and laughter in every moment of living with dogs (some messier than others). They offer life lessons to every human who takes the time to appreciate them, rather than judging them for being dogs.

REFERENCES

Kerns, Nancy. "Made in a Secret Location." *Whole Dog Journal,* January 2003, 6:1.

Salman, Dr. Mo (senior author). "Why Do Pets End Up In Shelters?" National Council on Pet Population Study and Policy, 1998, website: http://www.healthypet.com/library_view.aspx?ID=4.

AVSAB American Veterinary Society of Animal Behavior, 2008, website: http://www.avsabonline.org/avsabonline/images/stories/Position_Statements/puppy%20socialization.pdf.

Coppinger, Raymond and Lorna. *Dogs, A New Understanding of Canine Origin, Behavior, and Evolution.* The University of Chicago Press, 2001, p78, 170.

Diamond, Kathy. "Exercise, Why Dogs Need It." 2003, http://www.veterinarypartner.com/Content.plx?P=A&A=1396&S=1&SourceID=47.

Lindsay, Steven R. *Handbook of Applied Dog Behavior and Training Volume 3.* Blackwell Publishing, 2005, p407.

Blakeslee, Sandra. "If You Want to Know if Spot Loves You So, It's in His Tail." *New York Times,* 24 April 2007.

Scholz, Martina and Clarissa von Reinhardt, *Stress in Dogs.* Dogwise Publishing, 2007, p76.

RESOURCES

Recommended Reading

Aggressive Behavior in Dogs, James O'Heare, DogPsych Publishing, 2007. A comprehensive technical manual, written for dog behavior professionals.

The Allergy Solution for Dogs, Sean Messonnier, D.V.M. Prima Lifestyles, 2000. Learn the pros and cons of natural and conventional treatments.

Barking, the Sound of a Language, Turid Rugaas. Dogwise Publishing, 2008. Understanding barking and steps to minimize it.

Before and After You Get Your Puppy, Ian Dunbar. New World Library, 2004. A wonderful guide for those thinking about a puppy and what to do after the puppy comes home.

The Canine Aggression Workbook, James O'Heare. DogPsych Publishing 2007. An in-depth guide to understanding aggression and what to do about it.

The Culture Clash, Jean Donaldson. James and Kenneth, 2005. A fun book on understanding how your dog thinks and how to use that information to help your relationship with him.

Dogs, A New Understanding of Canine Origin, Behavior, and Evolution, Raymond Coppinger and Lorna Coppinger. University of Chicago Press, 2001. A no-nonsense book to understanding how dogs and humans came together and where that has led our relationships with dogs.

Don't Shoot the Dog!, Karen Pryor. Bantam, 1999. The book that help change the face of dog training toward modern, positive methods.

Food Pets Die For, Ann Martin. New Sage Press, 2003. The ins and outs of the pet food industry, and how to feed your dogs better.

Happy Kids, Happy Dogs, Barbara Shumannfang. Lulu Press, 2006. One of the most thoughtful books on dogs and kids living together—practical and thoughtful.

How to Right a Dog Gone Wrong, Pamela S. Dennison. Alpine Books, 2005. A straight-forward guide to help reactive dogs calm down and learn more acceptable behaviors.

On Talking Terms with Dogs, Calming Signals, Turid Rugaas. Dogwise Publishing, 2006. A fascinating and useful book for understanding how dogs communicate.

The Other End of the Leash, Why We Do What We Do Around Dogs, Patricia B. McConnell, Ph.D. Ballantine Books, 2002. A provocative look at the differences between humans and dogs.

Play Together, Stay Together, Patricia McConnell and Karen London. McConnell Publishing, 2008. How to use play for bonding and focus.

Play with Your Dog, Pat Miller. Dogwise Publishing, 2008. Miller explores the role and benefits of play between you and your dog—and between dogs. Play behaviors have important learning and health benefits that help dogs become well-adjusted members of both their canine and human families.

Positive Perspectives 2, Pat Miller. Dogwise Publishing, 2008. Pat Miller is one of the positive reinforcement pioneers and this volume is a collection of some of her best articles that were written for several publications. Everything from aggression to adoptions is covered.

Stress in Dogs, Martina Scholz and Clarissa von Reinhardt. Dogwise Publishing, 2007. The authors address and dissect the causes of stress and how it impacts the behavior of dogs.

Why Zebras Don't Get Ulcers, Robert M. Sapolsky. Owl Books, 2004. Cutting-edge research and humor bring together the science of stress and how it affects both two and four-legged animals.

The Wolf: The Ecology and Behavior of an Endangered Species, L. David Mech. University of Minnesota Press, 2003. The myths and truths about wolves and how different they are from domestic dogs.

Videos and DVDs

Clicker Magic, Karen Pryor, 2007. Learn all about clicker training and see firsthand its different applications including fish, horses, cats, and more.

Crate Games: For Self Control and Motivation, Susan Garrett, 2007. Teach your dog to love his crate with many useful and clever games to play with your dog.

The How of Bow Wow, Building, Proofing and Polishing Behaviors, Virginia Broitman, & Sherri Lippman, 2003. Dazzling behaviors, well filmed and easy to follow explanations for teaching your dog just about anything.

Calming Signals, What Your Dog Tells You, Turid Rugaas. Dogwise Publishing, 2005. The DVD that compliments the book, *On Talking Terms with Dogs.* Interesting and thought-provoking footage of dogs and how they communicate with us and one another.

Periodicals

Animal Wellness Magazine, 866-764-1212, www.animalwellnessmagazine.com.

Dog World Magazine, www.animalnetwork.com/DogWorldMag.

The Whole Dog Journal, 800-829-9165, www.whole-dog-journal.com.

Websites

www.avsabonline.org/avsabonline/images/stories/Position_Statements/puppy%20socialization.pdf. The American Veterinary Society of Animal Behavior Position Statement on early puppy socialization.

www.childwisdom.org/dietbehavior. This website contains lots of information about diet and behavior.

www.clickersolutions.com. A standard for everything "clicker."

www.clickertraining.com. Karen Pryor's website; the information offered there is considered the "Mecca" of clicker training.

www.doberdogs.com/menu.html. Dog food comparison charts.

www.dogaware.com. A good nutrition website that is very up to date on diet.

www.hollysden.com/say-no-to-shock-collars.htm. A compilation of what experts and others say about why not to use shock collars.

www.iaabc.org/articles/RKAnderson_PuppyVaccinationSocialization.pdf. A veterinarian's view on puppy vaccination and socialization.

www.monicasegal.com. Another good diet website.

pets.groups.yahoo.com/group/DogBeGood/. This is my Yahoo Group that brings together trainers and the public to help people understand their dogs and how to find positive only solutions to their problems.

www.topnotchdog.com/index.asp. A wonderful website dealing with kids and dogs.

www.ttouch.com. How to help your dog using Ttouch massage techniques and where to find a Ttouch Practitioner in your area.

www.trulydogfriendly.com/blog/?page_id=2. A group of trainers who are committed to positive only training and behavior modification techniques.

www.veterinarypartner.com. Exercise references.

www.wholedogtraining.com. My website.

Find a Behavior and/or Training Expert

Association of Pet Dog Trainers, www.apdt.com. A professional organization for trainers with lots of information available to the general public, including a listing of members.

International Association of Animal Behavior Consultants, www.iaabc.org. This is a professional association for the field of animal behavior consulting and has a world-wide referral service.

Karen Pryor Academy Find a Trainer, www.karenpryoracademy.com/find-a-trainer. All trainers have completed an extensive educational program with extremely high standards.

Products and Supplies

Books and DVDs, www.dogwise.com.

Calming Collars, www.calmingcollars.com/index.html. Handmade collars that help dogs calm down via an herbal mix in the collar.

Canine Auto Restraints, www.canineauto.com.

Car Ramps for Dogs, www.handiramp.com/Dog-Ramps/pet-ramps.htm.

Dog Restraints, www.ruffrider.com.

I-click and regular clickers and other training supplies, www.clickertraining.com.

Chew toys and treat dispensers, www.kongcompany.com.

Leashes and collars, www.gentleleader.com.

Treats and other supplies, www.sitstay.com.

Treat pouches and other low-cost products, www.upco.com.

Wholesome food and treats, www.welcometopawcountry.com.

Stress Test for Your Dog

Mark the box that best fits your dog.
Never = 1, Sometimes = 2, Usually = 3,
Most of the time = 4, Always = 5

Behavior	1	2	3	4	5
Dog is comfortable with all noises/sounds					
Dog is comfortable around all men					
Dog is comfortable around toddlers/babies					
Dog never jumps on people					
Dog loves attention from strangers if you are present					
Dog is comfortable being touched all over					
Dog is comfortable around all other dogs					
Dog is comfortable with delivery people					
Dog is comfortable being left with someone he knows					
Dog is comfortable being patted on the head					
Dog will eat no matter what is going on					
Dog is comfortable in crowds of people					
Dog will allow anyone to approach owner and remains friendly					
Dog never displays belly when people approach					
Dog allows hugs from strangers					
Dog never begs or barks for attention					
Dog is able to sleep while you are away from the home					
Dog rarely shows signs of stress via excess panting, yawning, sniffing, shaking, etc.					
Dog never growls or shows teeth to strangers					
Dog has never submissive urinated					
Dog never looks frightened when leaving the home					

Behavior	1	2	3	4	5
Dog never hides behind you when in public					
Dog never chews on or licks self excessively					
Dog doesn't tuck his tail when outside of home					

Answers:

Mostly 1-2's   Needs a stress reduction program.

Mostly 2-3's   Could use some behavior modification on the trouble areas.

Mostly 3-4's   Not too bad, but there are always ways to improve.

Mostly 4-5's   Good for you for having a relaxed dog!

Thirty Quick Ideas to Help You and Your Dog Relax When You Don't Have Time to Manage or Train your Dog

The following are 30 quick things you can do or plan for in response to your dog's behaviors when you are not really in the mood, or lack the time, to train him. These are a few ideas that will hopefully prevent reactions on your part, and instead, help you respond to the problem at hand with creative ways that relieve your own frustration and ultimately help your dog in the process. These "quick fixes" can help your dog while you are in the process of teaching him to relax.

1. Take a few slow, deep breaths! Not only will it help you relax, it will also show your dog that you are calm as you lead by example. This will also take some pressure off you and your pooch and allow you to think clearly about how to handle the situation.

2. Visit the Kong™ website and learn how to make many different Kongs that your dog will consider truly amazing and will keep him busy for awhile: http://www.kongcompany. com. If you make several magnificent Kongs ahead of time, you can freeze them and use them when you don't have time to make some from scratch.

3. Buy yourself some sanity—purchase baby gates, exercise pens, a crate, or other things help manage your dog's unwanted behaviors until you can train another behavior.

4. Step back for a moment and try to see things from your dog's point of view. Animals do what they do for good reasons (at least in their minds). There is a pay-off for doing what they do—it could be for safety, pleasure, attention, appetitive in nature, or just plain fun. Understand that dogs are not evil or vengeful, in fact, for the most part they try very hard to live in harmony with humans. When a dog misbehaves, it is his way of "telling" you he does not know the correct answer.

5. Buy yourself some dog walking time from a professional dog walker, or have a friend or family member take your dog out for a long walk or ride in the car.

6. Take two minutes a few times each day to teach your dog a cute trick using lots of treats—not only will you be giving your dog some mental exercise, it's hard to stay angry at a dog who is offering his paw, sitting pretty, or rolling over!

7. Buy a good steam cleaner. It's much easier to stay calm when your dog pukes on the new carpet if you can pull out the steam cleaner and make the mess go away quickly.

8. Take the time to sign up with a positive reinforcement trainer so you can learn more about teaching your dog manners. If you are already working with a trainer, call him and vent. Trainers also have bad days with their own companion animals and can lend an empathetic ear.

9. Buy your dog some doggie daycare time if he gets along with other dogs, or ask for a gift certificate for your next birthday, anniversary, etc.

10. Send your dog to the groomer, or have a mobile groomer come over—even if it's just for a bath. You will get some time away, and your pup will come back beautiful and clean.

11. Call and schedule a time to go out with a non-animal friend and don't talk about your dog! Everyone needs a break from living on Planet Pooch occasionally.

12. Buy your dog a wading pool and fill it with water and then drop Kongs stuffed with small amounts of peanut butter or spray cheese into the water so he can go fishing! Or, cut up turkey or chicken dogs and drop them in the water for your dog to fish out.

13. Buy a wading pool and turn it into a digging pit that you fill with dirt and sand, then bury lots of cool toys and treats so your dog can dig for buried treasures. This will keep your dog from digging the rest of the yard, especially if you keep "planting" really cool things for him to find in there. You can also give him a place in the yard to dig as well.

14. Buy a taste deterrent product to keep your dog from chewing on things that are not appropriate. There are several good ones sold at pet stores or online. (Be sure to reapply each day since these do fade in strength after they dry.)

15. Slow down with your dog in whatever you might be doing. Both you and he should take time to stop and smell the roses, admire the trees, and watch the birds or other things of interest, rather than hurrying through your time together.

16. Speed up with your dog; pick up the pace so he has to expend a little more energy, which will make him physically tired. This will also help to keep him focused on you since it's hard to move fast and pay attention to the world.

17. Change the routine for walks and exercise. If all you ever do is throw the ball for your dog, take a long walk. Alternatively, if you always take a walk around the block, go to a different neighborhood. Break up the routine. Your dog won't benefit from your outings if he doesn't have to think about them because they are mundane. Challenge his mind and body by trying new things and going to new places.

18. Take your dog for a car ride! Most dogs love to go in the car and what a treat if you don't go to the vet or groomers! You don't even have to go that far; around the block a couple of times can be pretty fun.

19. Give your dog permission to be messy! Let him have things that he can shred and chew such as a fast food restaurant hamburger in the bag so he has to rip and tear it open to get the hamburger. It's okay if he eats some small pieces of paper in the process—way better than many of the things he will find and eat during his lifetime.

20. Make a list of training goals for you and your dog, cross out all the ones that are unrealistic right now, and then pledge to work on the ones that are doable.

21. Give your dog something to chew that will take at least 30 minutes or longer, such as large rawhides, bully sticks, stuffed Kongs, or raw bones. Take a whole potato, poke lots of holes with a fork and boil in chicken broth, then freeze

it for a quick chew treat that dogs and puppies love. Chewing relieves stress and can give you some quiet time while your dog is busy.

22. Add something new to your dog's environment each day to provoke thought and interaction. Things that might be interesting to dogs: Cardboard boxes with toys and treats in them, old socks that are stuffed with treats and tied in knots, the core of toilet paper or paper towel rolls with a little paper left on them, oatmeal boxes with holes punched in them with treats and toys inside and the lid on, or an empty plastic bottle with your dog's whole meal in it (throw away the top), to name a few. Make a stop at a local thrift store or garage sale for other items. (Supervise all of these, of course!)

23. Take your dog's regular amount of food for one meal, cut up a few pieces of cheese or other high value treats, mix it together and toss it all out into the yard so he has to scavenge for his meal.

24. Make or buy a platform or ramp for your dog to climb on so he can watch the world from up high! This can be for inside or out. Or, cut a small peep hole in a gate or fence so he can see outside of his yard.

25. Breathe! Practice using calming behaviors with your dog to help him calm down: Take a number of deep breaths, yawn several times, avert your eyes, lick your lips while averting your eyes, and breathe some more! These calming behaviors can help you "talk" to your dog and aid in calming him.

26. Give in! Sometimes it is best to cut your losses and be okay with your dog doing what he is doing. Many pet parents have found that when they stop giving something so much attention, their dogs stopped caring so much about it.

27. Change your dog's food. Many impulse behaviors are calmed when dogs are switched from high-carbohydrate foods to high-end foods. Look for foods without corn, wheat, or soy products. In the end, these better foods will save you money

since you feed less and the real benefit is that they also create less waste!

28. Use a DAP Dog pheromone diffuser to help calm your dog. This plug-in device emits a scent is much like the pheromone that mother dogs secrete when nursing their puppies. It has a very calming effect.

29. Canine Lullabies has a CD that has a calming effect on dogs. (www.caninelullabies.com)

30. Laugh at, and with, your dog! Learn the wonderful lessons that dogs have to teach us everyday—most of which are about feeling good and not taking life so seriously.

INDEX

ABOUT THE AUTHOR

Nan Arthur, CDBC, CPDT, KPACTP has been involved in the behavior and training field for more than fifteen years with dogs and over twenty with cats. She has a deep belief that her mission is to help pet parents and their animals understand and communicate clearly with one another using the science of positive-only behavior and training methods.

Nan started her education and training in 1988 as a foster home for Friends of Cats in El Cajon, California. Several years later, she opened her home to foster dogs and cats from the San Diego County shelter system. Ultimately, Nan became a volunteer for the largest animal shelter in the San Diego area, affiliated with Friends of County Animal Shelters (FOCAS). After a short time, she was hired as the first Adoption Counselor with FOCAS.

Nan with Goldie

After five years with FOCAS and the San Diego Department of Animal Services, Nan was hired as the Senior Behavior Trainer of the San Diego Humane Society, and SPCA. She later added the title of Community Outreach Specialist, all the while designing and teaching many popular classes, including Feisty Fido, and her signature classes, "How to Live Happily Ever After with Your Dog or Cat" workshops and Puppy Fun Camp.

Nan started her own business, Whole Dog Training, after 4 years with the San Diego Humane Society. She now offers an array of public and private classes, as well as free and low-cost programs to the community, in her quest to help pets stay in their homes.

Nan, who is a faculty member and a Certified Training Partner with the Karen Pryor Academy, is also a 9-year member of the APDT, a Certified Pet Dog Trainer (CPDT), and a Certified Dog Behavior Consultant (CDBC) with the International Association of Animal Behavior Consultants, and holds many other certifications in the behavior and training field. She is a certified Veterinary Assistant, an award-winning writer and photographer, writes a weekly "Ask a Trainer" column for the East County Gazette in El Cajon, California, and freelances for magazines and other publications.

Nan and her husband Mike are the proud parents to two children, Sashie and Tiffanie. They are also pet parents to Pepper, Goldie, and Austin (dogs), and Billy Jean and Kelby (cats), all of whom came to their lives with special needs and gave the opportunity to learn more about animals.

BEHAVIOR & TRAINING

ABC's of Behavior Shaping. Proactive Behavior Mgmt, DVD set. Ted Turner

Aggression In Dogs. Practical Mgmt, Prevention, & Behaviour Modification. Brenda Aloff

Am I Safe? DVD. Sarah Kalnajs

Barking. The Sound of a Language. Turid Rugaas

Behavior Problems in Dogs, 3rd ed. William Campbell

Brenda Aloff's Fundamentals: Foundation Training for Every Dog, DVD. Brenda Aloff

Bringing Light to Shadow. A Dog Trainer's Diary. Pam Dennison

Canine Body Language. A Photographic Guide to the Native Language of Dogs. Brenda Aloff

Clicked Retriever. Lana Mitchell

Dog Behavior Problems. The Counselor's Handbook. William Campbell

Dog Friendly Gardens, Garden Friendly Dogs. Cheryl Smith

Dog Language, An Encyclopedia of Canine Behavior. Roger Abrantes

Evolution of Canine Social Behavior, 2nd ed. Roger Abrantes

From Hoofbeats to Dogsteps. A Life of Listening to and Learning from Animals. Rachel Page Elliott

Get Connected With Your Dog, book with DVD. Brenda Aloff

Give Them a Scalpel and They Will Dissect a Kiss, DVD. Ian Dunbar

Guide to Professional Dog Walking And Home Boarding. Dianne Eibner

Language of Dogs, DVD. Sarah Kalnajs

Mastering Variable Surface Tracking, Component Tracking (2 bk set). Ed Presnall

My Dog Pulls. What Do I Do? Turid Rugaas

New Knowledge of Dog Behavior (reprint). Clarence Pfaffenberger

Oh Behave! Dogs from Pavlov to Premack to Pinker. Jean Donaldson

On Talking Terms with Dogs. Calming Signals, 2nd edition. Turid Rugaas

On Talking Terms with Dogs. What Your Dog Tells You, DVD. Turid Rugaas

Play With Your Dog. Pat Miller

Positive Perspectives. Love Your Dog, Train Your Dog. Pat Miller

Positive Perspectives 2. Know Your Dog, Train Your Dog. Pat Miller

Predation and Family Dogs, DVD. Jean Donaldson

Really Reliable Recall. Train Your Dog to Come When Called, DVD. Leslie Nelson

Right on Target. Taking Dog Training to a New Level. Mandy Book & Cheryl Smith

Stress in Dogs. Martina Scholz & Clarissa von Reinhardt

Tales of Two Species. Essays on Loving and Living With Dogs. Patricia McConnell

The Dog Trainer's Resource. The APDT Chronicle of the Dog Collection. Mychelle Blake (*ed*)

The Dog Trainer's Resource 2. The APDT Chronicle of the Dog Collection.
Mychelle Blake (*ed*)
The Thinking Dog. Crossover to Clicker Training. Gail Fisher
Therapy Dogs. Training Your Dog To Reach Others. Kathy Diamond Davis
Training Dogs. A Manual (reprint). Konrad Most
Training the Disaster Search Dog. Shirley Hammond
Try Tracking. The Puppy Tracking Primer. Carolyn Krause
Visiting the Dog Park, Having Fun, and Staying Safe. Cheryl S. Smith
When Pigs Fly. Train Your Impossible Dog. Jane Killion
Winning Team. A Guidebook for Junior Showmanship. Gail Haynes
Working Dogs (reprint). Elliot Humphrey & Lucien Warner

HEALTH & ANATOMY, SHOWING
An Eye for a Dog. Illustrated Guide to Judging Purebred Dogs. Robert Cole
Annie On Dogs! Ann Rogers Clark
Another Piece of the Puzzle. Pat Hastings
Canine Cineradiography DVD. Rachel Page Elliott
Canine Massage. A Complete Reference Manual. Jean-Pierre Hourdebaigt
Canine Terminology (reprint). Harold Spira
Breeders Professional Secrets. Ethical Breeding Practices. Sylvia Smart
Dog In Action (reprint). Macdowell Lyon
Dogsteps DVD. Rachel Page Elliott
The Healthy Way to Stretch Your Dog. A Physical Theraphy Approach. Sasha
Foster and Ashley Foster
The History and Management of the Mastiff. Elizabeth Baxter & Pat Hoffman
Performance Dog Nutrition. Optimize Performance With Nutrition. Jocelynn Jacobs
Positive Training for Show Dogs. Building a Relationship for Success Vicki
Ronchette
Puppy Intensive Care. A Breeder's Guide To Care Of Newborn Puppies. Myra
Savant Harris
Raw Dog Food. Make It Easy for You and Your Dog. Carina MacDonald
Raw Meaty Bones. Tom Lonsdale
Shock to the System. The Facts About Animal Vaccination... Catherine O'Driscoll
Tricks of the Trade. From Best of Intentions to Best in Show, Rev. Ed. Pat Hastings
Work Wonders. Feed Your Dog Raw Meaty Bones. Tom Lonsdale
Whelping Healthy Puppies, DVD. Sylvia Smart

Dogwise.com is your complete source for dog books on the web!

2,000+ titles, fast shipping, and excellent customer service.